Cover illustration
A quiet, peaceful Dealey Plaza,
viewed from behind the picket
fence at the top of the grassy knoll.

Thanks to Kenneth F. Hersh
for the photograph.

THE JFK ASSASSINATION REVISITED

A Synthesis

James V. Rinnovatore & Allan Eaglesham

authorHOUSE®

AuthorHouse™
1663 Liberty Drive
Bloomington, IN 47403
www.authorhouse.com
Phone: 1-800-839-8640

Published by AuthorHouse 03/05/2014

ISBN: 978-1-4918-6496-8 (sc)
ISBN: 978-1-4918-6495-1 (hc)
ISBN: 978-1-4918-6494-4 (e)

Library of Congress Control Number: 2014902984

This book is printed on acid-free paper.

To
David S. Lifton and Douglas P. Horne
who illuminated the path to the truth

Other JFK-related works by the authors

"General" Activities at the Bethesda Morgue, 22 November 1963:
Posthumous words of an eyewitness lead to a new theory
(JVR & AE, 2012)
(http://www.manuscriptservice.com/McHugh/)

Aftermath of the JFK Assassination:
Parkland Hospital to the Bethesda Morgue
(JVR & AE, 2012)
(http://www.manuscriptservice.com/Aftermath/
and as an ebook from Amazon.com)

FBI Agents James W. Sibert and Francis X. O'Neill:
Analysis of their Activities at the Bethesda Morgue on November 22, 1963
(JVR &AE, 2011)
(http://www.manuscriptservice.com/JWS-FXO/)

Information on the Death of William Pitzer
(AE, 2011)
(http://www.manuscriptservice.com/PitzerFiles/)

JFK 11/22/63:
Who Took the Pre-Autopsy Photographs?
(JVR & AE, 2011)
(http://www.manuscriptservice.com/Pre-AutopsyPhotographs/)

Deep-Throat Dave
(AE & JVR, 2010)
(http://www.manuscriptservice.com/DeepThroat/)

JFK 11/22/63:
Where Was the Throat Wound Altered?
(JVR, 2010)
(http://www.manuscriptservice.com/Throat-Wound/)

JFK 11/22/63:
Body/Casket Chicanery at the Bethesda Morgue
(JVR, 2009)
(http://www.manuscriptservice.com/BNH-chicanery/)

The Untimely Death of LCDR William B. Pitzer:
Forensic Experts Examine the Evidence
(AE, 2009)
(http://www.manuscriptservice.com/WBP-Resolution/)

Where Were the JFK Autopsy Photographs Taken?
(AE, 2006)
(http://www.manuscriptservice.com/AutopsyRoom/)

The Untimely Death of William Bruce Pitzer, US Navy
(AE, 2005)
(http://www.manuscriptservice.com/Pitzer/)

(See also http://www.manuscriptservice.com/DarkCorners/)

Foreword

In a brief book published March, 2012, *Aftermath of the JFK Assassination: Parkland Hospital to the Bethesda Morgue*, [1] we provided a concise account, mainly of what transpired from 3:00 PM on November 22, 1963, when the body of President Kennedy left Parkland Memorial Hospital, to 8:00 PM, the starting time of the official autopsy at the National Naval Medical Center (NNMC), Bethesda.

We now provide a reformatting of the evidence in *Aftermath* to better support the fact that a break in custody of the body occurred during that 5-hour period, for the purpose of altering the wounds the president sustained in Dealey Plaza, Dallas. Also provided are discussions of:

- who planned the assassination,
- the investigative efforts of the Warren Commission, the House Select Committee on Assassinations (HSCA) and the Assassination Records Review Board (ARRB),
- who was responsible for taking the photographs of the president's wounds before alteration and when,
- the activities of FBI Agents James Sibert and Francis O'Neill at the Bethesda morgue,
- the autopsy photographs and X-rays,
- the supplementary autopsy report on the president's brain, and
- evidence that the extant Zapruder film is an altered document.

—James V. Rinnovatore & Allan Eaglesham
November 22, 2013

Acknowledgments

The authors thank Susanne Lipari, Bo Lipari, Kenneth Hersh and Mary Anne Rinnovatore for their comments and suggestions on the manuscript.

Contents

1. Context

At 2:38 PM (EST) on November 22, 1963, millions of Americans learned from Walter Cronkite that President Kennedy was dead. To say the least, this was shocking news, especially since he had been shot in public view while riding in a motorcade. Was it possible that a banana-republic-style assassination had taken place in our country? Was it possible that our much-loved president's young, vibrant life had been extinguished so horribly? Many of us found it inconceivable.

During the early evening of the day of the assassination, citizens, transfixed to their television sets for information, observed the arrival of Air Force One at Andrews Air Force Base near Washington, DC, at approximately 6:05 PM. The tail section opened and a bronze ornamental casket was off-loaded. Mrs. Kennedy and Bobby Kennedy, side-by-side, observed the lowering of the casket and its placement in a gray navy ambulance (Figure 1). Those in denial now knew for certain that John Fitzgerald Kennedy was no more, by observing his wife's blood-stained suit.

Mrs. Kennedy and her entourage entered the ambulance, which was part of a motorcade to the Bethesda Hospital, a division of the National Naval Medical Center (NNMC). Needless to say, she, as did the nationwide viewing audience, assumed that the president's body was in the ambulance. In fact, the casket was empty and the president's body, inside a body bag, was *en route* to the Bethesda morgue by helicopter. The removal of President Kennedy's body from the bronze casket, while *en route* to Andrews Air Force Base, was necessary to clandestinely take it to the morgue early, so that bullets could be removed and the wounds altered from what was observed and described by the doctors at Parkland Memorial Hospital, Dallas. The president had sustained wounds caused by shots from the front, whereas, in order to implicate Lee Harvey Oswald, the wounds had to appear as having been caused by shots from the rear. This was a key component to the cover-up of President Kennedy's assassination.

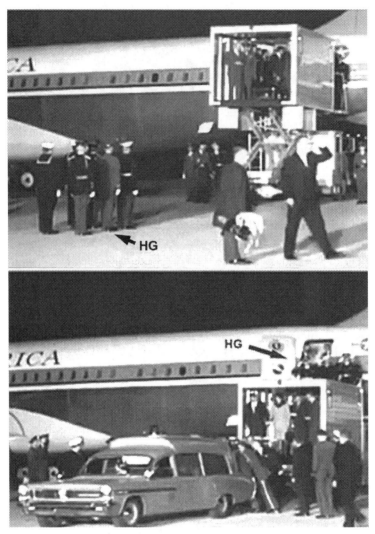

Figure 1. Air Force One at Andrews Air Force
Base. Upper: Casket about to be lowered.
Lower: Casket placed in the navy ambulance by some
members of the honor guard (HG) and others.

Author David Lifton made the astute observation many years ago in *Best Evidence* [2] that the president's body and his wounds—as observed by the doctors at Parkland Memorial Hospital in Dallas—were the "best evidence" for a true assessment of how President Kennedy was assassinated. The doctors at Parkland observed a wound in the anterior neck and in the right occipital (rear) region of the head. The latter wound was judged

2

to have been fatal. Descriptions of these wounds are contained in their contemporaneous reports. [3, Appendix VIII]

There was unanimity among the observations of the Parkland doctors: the president had sustained what appeared to be an entrance wound at the throat and an exit wound in the right-rear section of the skull. Wounds with these characteristics conform to frontal shots.

At 1:33 PM (CST) it fell to White House Press Secretary Malcolm Kilduff to announce the death of the president to members of the press assembled in a nurses classroom:

> President John F. Kennedy died at approximately one o'clock central standard time today here in Dallas. He died of a gunshot wound in the brain. I have no other detail regarding the assassination of the president.

Figure 2. Malcolm Kilduff: "...a bullet right through the head."

The hapless Kilduff was then peppered with questions, during which he stated, "Dr. Burkley[1] told me that it was a simple matter of a bullet right through the head," as he touched his forehead above the right eye (Figure 2).

These findings would, in due course, be contrary to the conclusions of the Warren Commission who determined that the president was shot from the rear by Lee Harvey Oswald, located in a sniper's nest of book cartons on the sixth floor of the Texas School Book Depository (TSBD).

---

[1]   Admiral George G. Burkley was President Kennedy's personal physician.

2. Evidence of a Conspiracy and Cover-Up

In all criminal cases, the chain-of-custody must be unbroken in order for items of physical evidence to be deemed valid at trial. Since the president's body was evidence in this case, it follows that once it was placed inside the ornamental bronze casket at Parkland Hospital, it should have traveled in an uninterrupted manner to the morgue at the NNMC, Bethesda, for autopsy. It did not. Therefore, the autopsy report should be considered circumspect, as it would in a court of law. Proof of interrupted travel between Dallas and Bethesda follows.

2.1. Early Arrival of the Body at the Bethesda Morgue

The official arrival time of the president's body at the morgue was approximately 8:00 PM, when the honor guard carried in the ornamental bronze casket. [4, p. 1] The honor guard—men from all five services—had also attended the arrival of the bronze casket at Andrews Air Force Base (Figure 1) and had traveled to Bethesda by helicopter.[4, p. 3] On the other hand, eyewitness accounts indicate that the body was carried into the morgue at 6:35/6:45 PM, [5, p. 3; 6, p. 5] *i.e.* before the gray navy ambulance carrying the bronze casket arrived in the motorcade from Andrews Air Force Base at the front entrance to the NNMC at 6:55 PM. [2, p. 407]

2.1.1. Eyewitnesses outside the morgue

In an interview with the Assassination Records Review Board (ARRB), **Dennis David**, chief-of-the day for the Naval Medical School (a division of the NNMC), said that he supervised a detail of sailors who removed a gray shipping casket from a "black hearse" at approximately 6:45 PM. This shipping casket was like those he observed frequently during the Vietnam War. [5, p. 3] Obviously, he was not describing the ornamental bronze casket taken into the morgue later by the honor guard. He also said that he observed arrival of a "motor cavalcade" that included a gray navy ambulance from which Mrs. Kennedy, Robert McNamara, and others alighted and entered the NNMC lobby. [5, p. 3] The motorcade arrived after he and his detail of sailors had taken the gray shipping casket into the "anteroom directly adjacent to the morgue." [5, p. 3] Chief David was not present when the shipping casket was opened; hence he had no firsthand knowledge of its contents. Being aware of the arrival of two caskets, on the following day he asked J. Thornton Boswell, one of the autopsy pathologists, which casket contained the president's body. Dr. Boswell replied, "You ought to know; you were there." [5, p. 3] Since David was at the morgue complex only when the gray shipping casket arrived, he took Boswell's response to imply that the body was in the shipping casket.

Marine Sergeant **Roger Boyajian** was in charge of a detail of marines who, from approximately 6:00 PM, were stationed at the morgue entrance to prevent unauthorized personnel from entering. In an after-action report [6], Sergeant Boyajian wrote: "At approximately 1835 (6:35 PM) the casket was received at the morgue entrance and taken inside." [6, p. 5] Boyajian did not describe the casket he observed entering the morgue at 6:35 PM. However, the fact that his time of entry was close to Chief David's estimated time of 6:45 PM, it is reasonable to presume that both men observed the same event: entry of a shipping casket. Additional corroboration is based on the account of four eyewitnesses who were inside the morgue at that time.

2.1.2. Eyewitnesses inside the morgue

In a telephone interview with Mark Flanagan, a staff member for the House Select Committee on Assassinations (HSCA)—X-ray technician **Edward Reed** said that he arrived in the morgue at approximately 6:30 PM. [7, p. 1] In his ARRB deposition, he stated that he found that, as he entered the hallway outside the morgue—at approximately 6:30 PM [7, p. 1]—a casket containing the president's body had already been delivered. He described a "typical military, aluminum casket, stainless steel or aluminum...lying on the ground" (*i.e.* floor) in the "hallway leading into the morgue" with "five or six Marine corpsmen at attention, lined up across the hallway." [8, pp. 21–26] Mr. Reed was likely describing some of the men in Boyajian's detail of marines. He helped carry the casket into the autopsy room and was present when it was opened. The body was "completely nude in a plastic bag." [8, p. 24]

In his deposition to the ARRB, photographer **Floyd Riebe** stated that he could not recall the time when "a gun-metal gray...very plain, inexpensive-type casket" was brought into the autopsy room. [9, pp. 27–29] However, he stated, "We were in the room for maybe half an hour before they brought the casket in." [9, p. 27]. The body "was in a rubberized-type body bag." [9, p. 30] He recalled that Paul O'Connor assisted in removing the body from the bag. [9, pp. 30–31]

In an interview conducted by the HSCA, technician **Paul O'Connor** described a "pink shipping casket," inside which the body was in a "body bag" [10, p. 2] He helped to unwrap a sheet from around the head and place the body on the autopsy table. [10, p. 3] In 1979, O'Connor told David Lifton that the body arrived in a "shipping casket," a "cheap...pinkish gray" casket that he likened to "a tin box." [2, pp. 598–599] The body was naked except for a sheet around the head. [2, p. 600]

2.2. Body Wrapping

Based on the Warren Commission testimony of Diana Bowron and Margaret Henchcliffe, nurses who helped to prepare the corpse for placement in the ornamental bronze casket at Parkland, the head and body were wrapped with sheets. [11, pp. 137, 141]. The fact that O'Connor observed only a sheet wrapped around the head indicates that the sheets around the body had been removed at some point—corroborating a break in the chain of evidence.

In 1979, medical technician James Metzler told David Lifton that he observed a regular viewing casket, or a ceremonial casket, being carried into the morgue by the honor guard [2, p. 631]. Metzler helped to place the body on the autopsy-room table; it was wrapped in two sheets—one around the body and one around the head. This account indicates that the wrappings on the body were changed twice after departure from Parkland at about 2:08 PM [12] and before arrival in the Bethesda morgue at 8:00 PM [4, p. 1], the importance of which cannot be overstated.

Having established that the president's body had been removed from the ornamental bronze casket at some point after it left Parkland Hospital and placed in a plain shipping casket prior to arrival in Bethesda, the question is why? One clear reason is that the wounds had to be altered, since they indicated shots from the front of the limousine.

3. The Wounds: Parkland Hospital vs. Bethesda Official Autopsy

3.1. Throat Wound

3.1.1. Parkland

In their testimony to the Warren Commission, Charles Carrico and Malcolm Perry, two of the first doctors to tend to President Kennedy in trauma room one, described the throat defect as small and circular, *i.e.* characteristics of an entry wound. Dr. Carrico said it was a "4–7-mm wound...rather round... no jagged edges..." [11, p. 3] Dr. Perry described it as "roughly circular or oval in shape, not a punched-out wound...roughly 5 mm in size..." [11, p. 9]

Although, according to Robert McClelland, President Kennedy was "comatose from a massive gunshot wound of the head" when he arrived at Parkland Hospital [3, p. 526], efforts were made to assist his breathing by insertion of a tracheostomy tube. To accommodate the tube, an incision of between 2 and 3 cm was made across the small throat wound by Malcolm Perry. [2, p. 272] Dr. McClelland described the incision as "smooth" and Paul Peters said it was "sharp." [2, p. 275] After the breathing tube had been removed, the incision made by Dr. Perry closed, revealing only the original small entry wound. Charles Crenshaw recalled:

> When the body left Parkland Memorial Hospital there was no gaping, bloody defect in the front of the throat, just a small bullet hole in the thin line of Perry's incision. [13, p. 54]

3.1.2. Bethesda

In stark contrast, when the president's body was observed at the start of the official autopsy, 8:00 PM, the thin line of Dr. Perry's incision across the throat was widened and elongated (Figure 3).

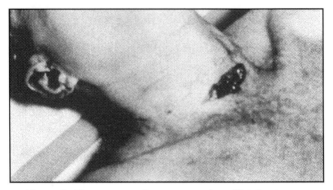

Figure 3. Throat wound as seen at the official autopsy.

In their report [3, p. 540], the autopsy doctors, James Humes, J. Thornton Boswell and Pierre Finck, described the throat wound as "a 6.5 cm long transverse wound with widely gaping irregular edges." In his Warren Commission testimony, Dr. Humes said it was "7 or 8 cm in length" (*i.e.* approximately 3 inches). [14, p. 361] Clearly, the 1-inch tracheotomy, made at Parkland, had been enlarged prior to the 8:00 PM autopsy at Bethesda.

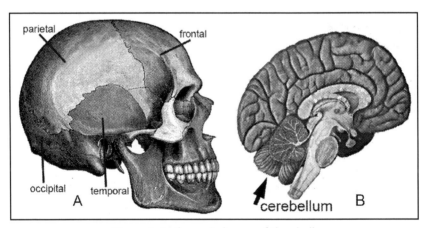

Figure 4. A: the main bones of the skull;
B: the location of the cerebellum.

3.2. Head Wound

3.2.1. Parkland

During his testimony to the Warren Commission, Dr. Carrico described the head wound as:

a large gaping wound, located in the right occipitoparietal area...about 5 to 7 cm in size, more or less circular, with avulsions[2] of the calvarium[3] and scalp tissue...I believe there was shredded macerated cerebral and cerebellar tissues both in the wounds and on the fragments of the skull attached to the dura[4]. [11, p. 6]

Figure 4A shows the location of the occipital and parietal bones. Figure 4B shows that the cerebellum is at the very base of the brain.

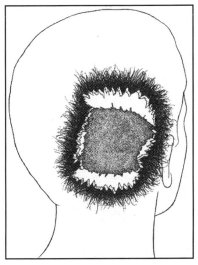

Figure 5. Representation of the head wound
as described by Robert McClelland.

Dr. McClelland told the Warren Commission: "I was in such a position that I could very closely examine the head wound, and I noted that the right posterior portion of the skull had been extremely blasted...in such a way that you could actually look down into the skull cavity itself and see that probably a third or so, at least, of the brain tissue, posterior cerebral tissue and some of the cerebellar tissue had been blasted out." [11, p. 33] For his book *Six Seconds in Dallas*, Josiah Thompson used McClelland's description to produce the illustration in Figure 5. [15, p. 107] With reference to this illustration, on January 24, 1994, Dr. McClelland wrote the following to

---

2   The forcible tearing away of a body part by trauma or surgery.
3   The domelike superior portion of the cranium.
4   The strongest and outermost of three membranes that protect the brain.

author Brad Parker: "[T]he drawing is an exact copy, in regard to location and dimensions, of the drawing I made for Josiah Thompson in 1966." [16] In his contemporaneous report, Kemp Clark, a neurosurgeon, described the head wound as "a large wound in the right occipitoparietal region...Both cerebral and cerebellar tissue were extruding from the wound." [3, p. 518] And in Dr. Perry's contemporaneous report [3, p. 521], the head wound was described as a "large wound in the right posterior cranium...exposing severely lacerated brain." These mutually consistent descriptions place the major wound in the right-rear section of the skull, with characteristics of an exit wound which, therefore, was caused by a frontal shot.

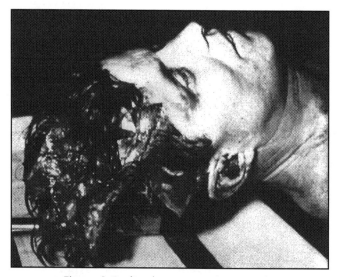

Figure 6. Bethesda autopsy photograph.

3.2.2. Bethesda

The autopsy report describes the head wound as "a large irregular defect of the scalp and skull on the right involving chiefly the parietal bone but extending somewhat into the temporal and occipital regions." Also, the defect "measures 13 cm in greatest diameter." [3, p. 540]

Upon comparison of the descriptions by the Parkland doctors with those in the autopsy report, we find that a defect of 5×7 cm, principally located in the occipito-parietal region (Parkland), had increased to a 13-cm defect principally located in the parietal region (Bethesda autopsy): the rear head wound had "moved" to the top of the head and become larger (Figure 6).

The conflicting descriptions between Parkland and Bethesda are so stark that it is impossible to attribute them to either incompetence or human error.

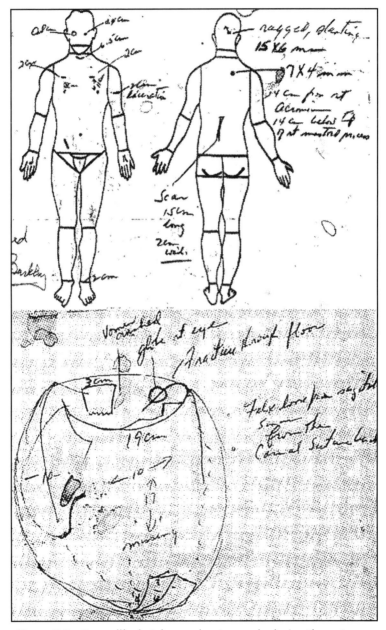

Figure 7. Dr. Boswell's sketches and notes made during the autopsy.

In describing the damage to the skull in the autopsy face sheet (Figure 7), Dr. Boswell wrote:

- "Vomer crushed" (*i.e.* the bone in the nose was fractured)
- "globe rt. eye Fracture through floor" (*i.e.* the bone around the right eye was fractured)
- "Falx loose from sagittal sinus from the coronal suture back" (*i.e.* the fold in the dura was loose posterior to the coronal suture, see Figure 8).

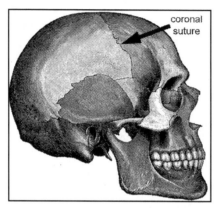

Figure 8. Location of the coronal suture.

The notation "10x17" (in centimeters) (Figure 7) represented an area in which most of the skull bone was missing. The number 19 represented nineteen centimeters of fragmented frontal bone. The "3 cm" notation above the left eye represented cracked bone in that location. And "10" on the left represented the size of a bone (in centimeters) broken away from the skull, but still attached to the scalp. [17, pp. 69–70]

It is inconceivable that the damage to the top of the head, as described by Boswell, would not have been noticed by the Parkland doctors. And if the falx membrane were extruded from the skull cap, it is likely that it would have been observed at Parkland. Since none of the Dallas doctors wrote of such damage in their contemporaneous reports, it is reasonable to conclude that it was not there.

A question should be raised at this point: Why weren't Dr. Boswell's descriptions included in the autopsy report? We believe that the omission was intentional to minimize questions being raised *vis-à-vis* more damage to the president's skull, as described by Boswell, than what was described by the Parkland doctors. In effect, Dr. Boswell's observations, which should have been the same as seen by Dr. Humes, were too much for Humes to include in his autopsy report lest they raise red flags.

3.3. Back Wound

3.3.1. Parkland

With the possible exceptions of Marion Jenkins [18, p. xxvi] and Diana Bowron, [18, p. 183] no one at Parkland saw the back wound. Nurse Bowron noticed it on washing the body, in preparation for placement in the bronze ornamental casket.

3.3.2. Bethesda

Dr. Boswell also made notes and sketches describing the back wound as seen at the official autopsy (Figure 7, *i.e.* the autopsy face sheet). Of particular interest is where Boswell placed the back wound, which he annotated as "7×4 mm." He wrote that this defect was "14 cm from rt Acromion 14 cm below tip of rt mastoid process." The acromion is part of the shoulder blade; the mastoid process is a conical protuberance at the lowest point of the temporal bone (Figure 9). On the face sheet, he placed the back wound well below the shoulder and, therefore, below the throat wound. If the throat and back wounds resulted from the passage of a single bullet, then, based on Boswell's locations, one would conclude that the bullet had been fired from the trunk of the limousine, which, obviously, did not happen. In other words, the throat wound and the back wound were unconnected. Clearly, Boswell's observations were in sharp disagreement with Humes' conclusion in the autopsy report that the back and throat wounds resulted from a single shot fired from above and behind the president.

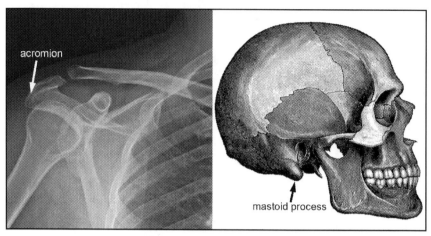

Figure 9. Reference points used by Dr. Boswell to
describe the location of the back wound.

During Dr. Boswell's deposition to the ARRB, Jeremy Gunn asked about
his placement of the back wound, the "7x4 mm" notation in the face
sheet (Figure 7): "I'd like to ask you a question now about the thoracic
wound that is on right diagram... Do you see that?" Boswell replied, "It's
not thoracic, though...it's neck." [17, p. 72] Continuing discussion of the
back wound, Gunn asked, "How would you describe it?" to which Boswell
replied, "It's neck." [17, p. 72] Gunn then showed Boswell what was written
on page 3 of the autopsy report: "Situated on the right posterior thorax
just above the upper border of the scapula there is a 7-by-4 millimeter
oval wound." Gunn then asked, "Could you explain to me what it means
that the wound was situated on the upper right posterior thorax?" Boswell
replied:

> *Well, that's what the diagram is meant to depict. Posterior
> thorax—upper right posterior thorax would be there in that
> general area. But then the numbers indicate its position
> much better, and Jim wrote, 'just above the upper border of
> the scapula.' Well, the scapula is this whole shoulder girdle
> here, and so it has to be up above here. And then it says '14
> centimeters below the tip of the right mastoid process.' Well,
> the mastoid process is not delineated on here, but it's just at the
> ear. So 14 centimeters really would be down here at the base of
> the neck. [17, pp. 72–73]*

Gunn followed up by showing Boswell the death certificate that had been signed by George Burkley [19] and asked if he had ever seen it. When Boswell replied, "No," he was asked to read what Dr. Burkley had written on page two: "President Kennedy...was struck in the head by an assassin's bullet and a second wound occurred in the posterior back at about the level of the *third thoracic vertebra*." [emphasis added] The location of the third thoracic vertebra is shown in Figure 10.

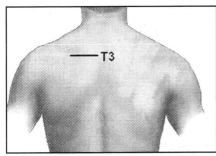

Figure 10. Location of the third thoracic vertebra.

Gunn asked Boswell whether Dr. Burkley was correct with the location of the back wound at the third thoracic vertebra. Boswell replied, "No...It would not be a thoracic vertebra. It would have to be a cervical vertebra," [17, p. 74] and added:

When we saw the clothing, we realized that where I had drawn this was—if you looked at the back of the coat, it was in the exact same place. But the coat had been—was up like this. He was waving and this was all scrunched up like this. And the bullet went through the coat way below where this would be on his body, because it was really at the base of his neck. And the way I know this best is my memory of the fact that—see, we probed this hole which was in his neck with all sorts of probes and everything, and it was such a small hole, basically, and the muscles were so big and strong and had closed the hole and you couldn't get a finger or a probe through it.

But when we opened the chest and we got at—the lung extends up under the clavicle and high just beneath the neck here, and the bullet had not pierced through into the lung cavity but had caused hemorrhage just outside the pleura. And so if I can move this up to here—it's shown better on the front, actually. The wound came through and downward just above the thoracic cavity and out the thyroid cartilage. So if you put a probe in this and got it back through like this, that would come out right at the base of the neck. [17, pp. 75–76]

Dr. Boswell was engaging in pure gobbledygook as well as stretching the truth. His placement of the back wound (Figure 7) corresponds closely to the level of the third thoracic vertebra (T3) (Figure 10). Certainly, he could not have made such a gross error between the neck and the back when he was looking at the body. His verbiage about the clothing and how the clothes were "all scrunched up" is nonsensical. The issue here is the location of the wound on the body, not the location of holes in the clothing. In their FBI report, James Sibert and Francis O'Neill described the wound as "a bullet hole which was below the shoulders and two inches to the right of the midline of the spinal column." [20, p. 4] The FBI agents wrote what the pathologists were describing: the wound was in the back, not in the neck. In addition, Sibert and O'Neill described the trajectory and degree of penetration of the bullet in question:

> *This opening was probed by Dr. Humes with the finger, at which time it was determined that the trajectory of the missile entering at this point had entered at a downward position of 45 to 60 degrees. Further probing determined that the distance travelled by this missile was short, inasmuch as the end of the opening could be felt with the finger.* [20, p. 4]

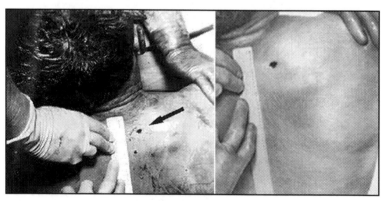

Figure 11: Autopsy photograph (arrow added) and
illustration by Ida Dox[5] of the back wound.

This description by Sibert and O'Neill is consistent with:

---

[5]   Medical illustrator who copied autopsy photographs for viewing by the HSCA.

- the apparent bullet wound in the autopsy photograph shown in Figure 11,
- the location of the back wound indicated by Boswell on the face sheet (Figure 7),
- Burkley's estimate that the back wound was at the level of the third thoracic vertebra (Figure 10), [19, p. 2] and
- the "official" placement of the back wound by Ida Dox for the HSCA (Figure 11).

The arrow in Figure 11 indicates the wound of entrance described by Humes in his deposition to the ARRB. [21, pp. 165–168] When asked the purpose of the ruler, Humes replied, "Just to record visually the size of the wound [21, p. 166]. When asked if the mark that "appears to be high at approximately the second-centimeter line (on the ruler) identifies the wound of entry," he responded, "Yes, sir." [21, p. 167] We placed the arrow at about 2 cm from the top of the ruler.

Even with Dr. Humes' placement of the back wound—about which we have reservations (discussed in Section 9.1.7.2.)—clearly, it is below the throat wound. Humes should have been questioned further about this placement since it does not agree with where he placed the back wound in the autopsy report. Furthermore, he should have been asked why this photograph does not show the head wound in the right-rear area seen by doctors at Parkland Hospital (*e.g.* see Figure 5).

4. Alterations of the Wounds: When, Where and by Whom?

The accounts of eyewitnesses provide direct proof that the wounds—head and throat—were altered by Dr. Humes shortly after the body entered the Bethesda morgue in a shipping casket, at 6:35/6:45 PM. Also, indirect photographic evidence indicates that the alterations were performed at the Bethesda morgue.

4.1. Direct Evidence

- **Jerrol Custer** took the X-rays of the body at the Bethesda morgue. His deposition to the ARRB included the following comments: "There was more than one casket that night...There was a casket brought in the back by a black Cadillac ambulance. Plus, there was a casket that Jacqueline Kennedy had in her entourage, too." [22, p. 72] His account of a "black Cadillac" conforms to Dennis David's account that a shipping casket had been removed from a black Cadillac. [2, p. 575]

  When asked about the body's appearance when he first observed it, Custer replied, "What surprised me, he had a plastic bag around his head with sheets wrapped around it. And you could see the blood on the sheets...and after we got him on the table, I was asked to leave." [22, p. 80]

  Upon his return to the morgue, Custer observed damage to the head in the parietal-temporal region [22, pp. 92–93]. A section of bone between the temporal and parietal areas, on the right side of the head was "flapped out. It looked as if they had sawed it." [22, p. 96] This damage did not exist at the time the president's body was tended to at Parkland.

  Custer's observations of the throat wound are also revealing. At some point, he observed the throat wound to be "a little bit bigger than my little finger...in diameter." [22, p. 90] It is likely that he made this observation before he left the morgue. When asked if he had noticed a long incision or cut on the throat, he replied, "Not at that time, I didn't." [22, p. 90] It is plausible that Custer did, in fact, see a much larger cut across the throat on his return to the morgue, after alterations had been made.

- **Edward Reed** assisted Custer in taking X-rays during the official autopsy. In his deposition to the ARRB, when asked to describe the first incision on the body, he replied, "And Commander Humes made an incision...in the forehead, and brought back the scalp...After about 20 minutes Commander Humes took out a saw and started to cut the forehead with the bone—with the saw. Mechanical saw. Circular, small, mechanical..." [8, pp. 57–58] Reed was then asked to leave the morgue. [8, p. 59] There is no description of this event in the autopsy report leading one to presume it occurred before the official autopsy began. The authors believe that Dr. Humes' use of a saw, which Reed described, was done to remove evidence of a frontal shot to the right side of the forehead. Asking Reed (and Custer) to leave the morgue just as the alterations were begun was to ensure they would not be eyewitnesses to the alteration process.

- **John Stringer** was the principal photographer of the autopsy at the Bethesda morgue. In a telephone interview with HSCA staff members Jim Kelly and Andy Purdy, Stringer stated that "the doctors had to crack the skull to get the brain out...they didn't have to saw it off." [23, p. 17] Cracking the skull—a highly unusual procedure to remove the brain—was not mentioned in the autopsy report. Moreover, no witness at the official autopsy (after 8:00 PM) described activity on the part of the prosectors that involved cracking of the skull. Therefore, it follows that this was done before the start of the official autopsy. The second reason this bears significance is that the standard protocol in any autopsy to remove the brain is to saw the top off the cranium. Cracking the skull would create damage beyond what was originally caused by the bullet(s), in effect masking the evidence of the original wound(s).

- **Thomas Robinson** was a mortician with Gawler's funeral home, the service that embalmed the president's body and reconstructed the head for possible viewing. In his interview with HSCA staff members Andy Purdy and Jim Conzelman, Robinson described a defect located on the right side of the head "at the temples [sic] in the hairline...a quarter inch in size." [24, pp. 2–3] This is characteristic of an entry wound. It was not discussed in the autopsy report.

- **FBI Agents Sibert and O'Neill** took notes of the statements made by chief pathologist Humes during the official autopsy, which began at 8:00 PM. They subsequently wrote a report [20; Appendix I). Shortly after 8:00 PM—at which time the ornamental bronze casket was brought into the morgue by the honor guard—Dr. Humes made the following statement:

  Following the removal of the wrapping, it was ascertained that the President's clothing had been removed and it was also apparent that a tracheotomy had been performed, as well as surgery of the head area, namely, in the top of the skull. [20, p. 3]

  His comment about "surgery of the head area" was significant since no surgery had been performed at Parkland. It begs the question of the type of surgery he was referring to. In addition, we believe that his characterization of the gross wound in the throat (Figure 3) simply as a "tracheotomy" was intended to be misleading.

- A review of Dr. Humes' autopsy report might be helpful. For example, the section titled "MISSILE WOUNDS" [3, p. 540] states:

  1. There is a large irregular defect of the scalp and skull on the right involving chiefly the parietal bone but extending somewhat into the temporal and occipital regions. In this region there is an actual absence of scalp and bone producing a defect which measures approximately 13 cm. in greatest diameter.

> From the irregular margins of the above scalp defect tears
> extend in stellate fashion into the more or less intact scalp as
> follows:
>
> > a. From the right inferior temporo-parietal margin
> > anterior to the right ear to a point slightly above the
> > tragus[6].
> > b. From the anterior parietal margin anteriorly on the
> > forehead to approximately 4 cm. above the right orbital
> > ridge.
> > c. From the left margin of the main defect across the midline
> > antero-laterally for a distance of approximately 8 cm.
> > d. From the same starting part as c. 10 cm. postero-
> > laterally.

According to Humes, the four tears in the scalp—a, b, c and d, above—
formed a "stellate" (star-shaped) pattern, which begs the question of how
such a pattern of tears was produced by a bullet. A plausible explanation is
that the "tears" were incisions made by Humes before the official autopsy,
to gain access to the inner recesses of the brain. His stated observation
of surgery to the head was a ruse to deceive FBI Agents Sibert and O'Neill
who, up to that time, had been absent from the autopsy room. [25, p. 242]
Dr. Humes had to be accurate as to what he was observing while, at the
same time, concealing the alterations of the wounds that he himself had
made earlier. Likewise for his statement about the tracheotomy. He was
well aware that he had expanded, in crude fashion, the 1-inch tracheotomy.
His implication that they were looking at a standard tracheotomy was
made to fool the FBI agents into believing that the 3-inch gash had been
made at Parkland Hospital, Dallas.

4.2. Indirect Evidence

- **Saundra Spencer** was in charge of the "White House Photo Lab"
  at the Naval Photographic Interpretation Center in Anacostia.
  In a telephone interview with the ARRB [26], she stated that,
  on November 23, 1963, she received three or four duplex film
  holders (six or eight sheets of film comprising color negatives)
  from a "federal agent." [26, p. 2]. She understood these negatives

---

6   Small, pointed eminence of the external ear, projecting backward.

to have been exposed at the autopsy and offered the following observations regarding the prints that she made: [26, p. 3]

- The body was "very clean"—"no blood and no gore"—unlike in other autopsy photographs she had seen.
- A circular wound at the base of the neck was about the size of a person's thumb in breadth.
- A wound in the back of the head, at about the center, 3 or 4 inches above the hairline, was 2 to 2½ inches wide: a "blown out chunk."

It is almost certain that the prints Ms. Spencer developed showed the wounds as they existed at Parkland Hospital, *i.e.* before alterations. Evidently, the "very clean" body had been washed prior to taking the photographs. This is consistent with photographer John Stringer's testimony to the ARRB that the body was washed before he took photographs. [27, p. 161].

After developing the negatives and making prints, she gave all the material to the federal agent, who, she believed, was named Fox[7].

Spencer's observations of the wounds are particularly significant because photographs were taken of the body only in the Bethesda autopsy room. Since photographs were taken of the wounds before they were altered (per Ms. Spencer's descriptions), as well as after alterations (including those shown in Figures 3 and 6), and since all photographs of the body were taken in the Bethesda autopsy room, it follows that the alterations of the throat and head wounds were made in the Bethesda morgue by Dr. Humes.

When Humes first observed the body at 6:35/6:45 PM, the throat wound must have appeared to him as it did to Saundra Spencer—a circular wound about the size of a person's thumb.

---

[7] Possibly James K. Fox, photographer with the Intelligence Division of the Secret Service and source of "bootlegged" copies of Kennedy-autopsy photographs (including those in Figures 3 and 6). [28]

- **Dr. Humes'** subsequent phone calls (there were two within a brief period [29, p. 380]) to Malcolm Perry—on the day after the assassination [29, p. 380]—about the throat wound and whether surgery had been performed by him (Perry) was another ruse by Humes, a cover story. During the first conversation, according to notes made by Humes (Figure 12) [30]), Perry gave Humes details of the throat wound: "only a few mm in size 3–5 mm" with "injury to rt. lat. wall of the trachea" and "no missle [sic] in the wound." Perry confirmed in detail what Humes had been told by Robert Livingston even before the arrival of Air Force One at Andrews Air Force Base: the president had received a bullet wound to the throat. [31, p. 170] However, Humes pretended that Perry's information was news to him, that Perry's 1-inch tracheotomy had obscured the throat wound such that he (Humes) was unaware of its existence. He told the ARRB:

  > ...early the next morning, I called Parkland Hospital and talked with Malcolm Perry, I guess it was. And he said, 'Oh, yeah, there was a wound right in the middle of the neck by the tie, and we used that for the tracheotomy.' Well, they obliterated, literally obliterated [the bullet wound in the throat]... [21, p. 36]

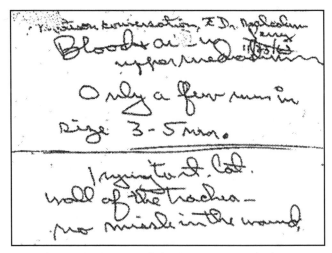

Figure 12. Notes made by James Humes during a phone call with Malcolm Perry on 11/23/63. [30]

4.3. Who?

As to why photographs were taken of the president's original wounds is anybody's guess. In any event, they have disappeared along with many other photographs taken during the official autopsy. Floyd Riebe recalled that he took approximately a hundred black and white photographs [9, p. 41] and John Stringer recalled that the took forty to fifty color and black and white photographs. [27, p. 126] The question is: who took the photographs of the president's unaltered wounds?

5. The Pre-Autopsy Photographs

We will provide evidence that John Stringer, the official autopsy photographer, took photographs of the wounds before alterations, during a time designated as the "pre-autopsy," *i.e.*between approximately 6:40 PM (arrival of the gray shipping casket), and approximately 8:00 PM when the honor guard carried the ornamental bronze casket into the morgue.

5.1. Messrs. Stringer and Riebe

John Stringer was the photographer of record and Floyd Riebe his assistant during the official autopsy. [23, pp. 10, 11] Mr. Stringer, a civilian, was director of medical photography at the Naval Medical School (a division of the NNMC), under the supervision of John Stover. [23, p. 9] Mr. Riebe, a hospital corpsman second class, was a student in the medical photography school, where some of his classes had been taught by Mr. Stringer. [9, p. 7]

On the afternoon of 11/22/63, after receiving official word from the chief of the day, Riebe called Stringer at home to advise him that the autopsy on President Kennedy's body was to be done at Bethesda. [9, p. 21] Riebe gathered film, cameras, and other equipment, [9, p. 22] and subsequently went to the main entrance to identify Stringer so that he could enter the hospital complex. [9, pp. 21–22] Stringer then asked Riebe to procure a strobe unit (electronic flash). [9, p. 24] Presumably, Riebe took the strobe to the autopsy room where Stringer was waiting.

In a telephone interview in 1977, Stringer told HSCA staff members Jim Kelly and Andy Purdy that he received a telephone call from Dr. Humes, who told him to come into work. [23, p. 9] Kelly and Purdy reported that Stringer stated that he was "present in the room where the autopsy was conducted between approximately 6:00 and 6:30 PM on the night of the 22nd and 3:00 to 3:30 AM on the morning of the 23rd." [23, p. 12]

In his ARRB deposition, Mr. Riebe stated, "We were in the room for maybe half an hour before they brought the casket in," [9, p. 27] which indicates a 6:05/6:15 PM arrival time. Since he had been describing their interaction, it follows that his use of "we" included Stringer, indicating that both men were in the autopsy room when the gray shipping casket with the president's body arrived at 6:35/6:45 PM. Thus, Riebe confirmed Stringer's recollection, expressed to the HSCA staff, that he (Stringer) arrived at about 6:15 PM. [23, p. 12] Riebe described a "very plain, inexpensive type casket" and that the body was "in a rubberized-type body bag." [9, pp. 29–30] In his deposition to the ARRB, Stringer said he was in the morgue when the body arrived, [27, p. 66] describing the casket in vague terms as "metal" and "I think it was sort of brownish." [27, p. 67] Unfortunately, he was not pressed to provide a more precise description of the casket. If, as Stringer claimed, he entered the autopsy room sometime between 6:00 and 6:30 PM, it is reasonable to conclude that he witnessed not only two entries of the body—first in a body bag within a shipping casket, as described by Riebe, [9, pp. 29–30] and later in the ceremonial bronze casket—but also the chicanery that was necessary to replace the body in the ceremonial casket, after the pre-autopsy, and temporarily remove it from the autopsy room. [1]

We agree with Doug Horne [32, p. 1003] and interpret Stringer's "metal/brownish" vagueness as a wish to imply that he witnessed only the arrival of the ceremonial bronze casket, finessing the fact that he had also witnessed the arrival of the shipping casket/body bag.

When asked how much time elapsed after the body was taken out of the casket before he began taking photographs, Stringer replied, "Oh, it must have been more than an hour by the time they took the X-rays. And they had to develop them and bring them back down." [27, pp. 66–67] We view this response as an obfuscation intended solely to answer the question as it applied to the official autopsy, which began at about 8:00 PM, while hiding the fact he took the pre-autopsy photographs much earlier. It is known that X-rays were still being taken after prosector Pierre Finck arrived at the morgue at approximately 8:30 PM. [33, pp. 70, 76] And taking account of the time required to develop the film and examine them, X-raying was likely completed at approximately 9:30 PM. Thus, Mr. Stringer's response gives the impression that he started taking photographs at about 9:30 PM. If so, what had he been doing since he entered the autopsy room at 6:15 PM? We believe that he evaded the question as to when he started taking photographs so as to avoid, again, the controversial subject of the arrival of the shipping casket/body bag, which he witnessed.

5.2. Cracking the Skull

Evidence additional to that elucidated in Section 4.1.—*i.e.* Stringer's account to Kelly and Purdy that "the doctors had to crack the skull somewhat to get the brain out...they didn't have to saw it off" [23, p. 17]—corroborates Stringer's presence during the pre-autopsy phase. Two anecdotal accounts are consistent with his description of the skull being cracked:

- "Mutilation of three bullet punctures to the head area," [34, p. 1] and
- A ball-peen hammer being used on the head. [35]

5.3. Throat-Wound Examination

In his ARRB deposition, John Stringer stated that a metal probe was placed in the neck wound, front to back. [27, pp. 191–192] There is no discussion in the official autopsy report—or description by others present at the official autopsy of insertion of a metal probe—into the throat wound. Technicians Paul O'Connor and James Jenkins, who were present during the official autopsy, described insertion of probes into the back wound, [25, pp. 40, 74] but both men made it clear that the throat wound was not probed:

> **O'Connor**: *We weren't able to do certain critical things like probe the throat wound that we thought was a bullet wound. We found out it was a bullet wound years later.* [25, p. 45]

> **Jenkins**: (When asked, "Did anybody tell you not to probe the throat wound?") *No, because we went through the whole autopsy on the premise that the throat wound was a trach.* [25, p. 78]

Not only was Stringer present when a metal probe was inserted into the throat, but he made the shocking declaration to the ARRB that he saw "the doctor" insert his fingers into the "tracheotomy wound" in an attempt to find bullet fragments. [27, p. 191] Given that a standard tracheotomy had been performed at Parkland Hospital, producing a wound of about an inch in length, the incision must have been enlarged to accommodate digital probing.

Although Floyd Riebe was assisting Stringer, he did not witness probing of the throat simply because he was asked to leave the morgue soon after arrival of the body in the shipping casket. [9, p. 32] The only probing Mr. Riebe recalled was of the back wound by Dr. Finck, [9, p. 38] who arrived in the autopsy room at about 8:30 PM. [33, p. 70]

It is noteworthy that Riebe indicated to the ARRB that, after he had started taking general body photographs, "X-ray came in and we had to leave." [9, p. 32] The use of "we" indicates that he and Stringer left the autopsy room at that stage. However, based on our previous discussion regarding Stringer's witnessing cracking of the president's skull and probing of the wounds with fingers and metal rods, we suggest that if Stringer left the morgue with Riebe, he returned shortly thereafter. Mr. Stringer's observations—not witnessed by Messrs. Riebe, O'Connor or Jenkins, and not described in the autopsy report—must have been made during the pre-autopsy timeframe.

If the throat wound were simply a tracheotomy, which Dr. Humes insisted was his belief throughout the autopsy, [21, p. 76] it begs the question of why a metal probe was inserted, with digital manipulation to find bullet fragments. In his ARRB deposition, when asked, "Did you take any action at Bethesda that increased the size of the tracheotomy?" Humes provided this literally incredible response: "I don't think so. I don't believe so." [21, p. 174] If, as Doug Horne has suggested, Humes officiated at the pre-autopsy, [32, pp. 1004, 1169] then Humes must have known that the tracheotomy had been made over a bullet wound. That he did not treat the throat wound as such during the official autopsy indicates that he fully understood that it was a wound of entry, consistent with the claim by Robert Livingston that he (Livingston) advised Humes of the existence of the throat wound prior to 6:00 PM. [31, p. 170]

5.4. Robert Knudsen

Although Mr. Stringer didn't think that he took photographs of the probe in the neck, [27, p. 192] White House photographer Robert Knudsen, in a deposition to the HSCA, corroborated Stringer's description of the metal neck probe when he described developing a negative depicting probes through the president's body, one through the chest and one through the neck. [36, pp. 31–35] Furthermore, the negative showed that the thorax was held erect [36, p. 35] indicating that no "Y"-incision had been made at the time of the probing, otherwise the body would not have been erected; this points to a pre-autopsy timeframe. In fact, in none of the negatives or prints processed by Knudsen had the chest been opened. [36, p. 40]

When asked when he first became aware of the existence of photographs of the autopsy of the president, Mr. Knudsen replied, "The morning following the autopsy." [36, p. 5] Therefore, according to his HSCA testimony, Knudsen did not take photographs during the pre-autopsy or during the official autopsy.

The possibility of Robert Knudsen being the photographer during the pre-autopsy has been discussed by Doug Horne. [32, pp. 904, 905, 906, 1003 n3] Mr. Horne indicated that one fact negating this possibility is that Mr. Knudsen told his son that he arrived at the Bethesda Hospital from Andrews Air Force Base via the motorcade, at about 6:55 PM. [32, p. 1003 n3] Horne concluded that this arrival time would not have been early enough for Knudsen to take photographs of the president's original wounds (before alterations). We agree, and believe that additional factors negate this possibility. Knudsen was a social photographer, who had never even seen autopsy photographs. [36, p. 32] Nor was he stationed at the NNMC.

Setting aside that Knudsen told his son that he arrived at the hospital in the motorcade from Andrews Air Force Base, Horne offered the possibility that Knudsen rode in a Gawler's funeral home hearse from Andrews to Bethesda. [32, p. 1004 n3] Although this might have allowed Knudsen to arrive early enough to take the initial photographs, there is no evidence that a Gawler's hearse was at Andrews Air Force Base. According to Joe Hagen, a manager at Gawler's, an original order was rescinded; they were directed not to go to Andrews. [32, p. 591] The Gawler's personnel were told that the body/casket would be transported from Andrews by navy ambulance. [32, p. 591] It is known now that the bronze casket placed in a navy ambulance at Andrews AFB was empty. The body was transported by helicopter, [32, p. 591 n2] which accounts for its arrival at the NNMC before the navy ambulance arrived from Andrews.

None of the photographs shown to Knudsen by HSCA staff member Purdy depicted probes. Moreover, toward the end of the deposition, Purdy said:

> *Also, there has not been previous evidence that there were either metal probes that were extended totally through the body, or that such probes were photographed through the body.* [36, p. 51]

The suggestion that Knudsen was mistaken elicited uncertainty in his responses, of which the following are particularly revealing:

> *Why this* [film depicting probes] *sticks in my mind that there was one with these two probes through the body that nobody else recalls, it puts a question in my mind, and yet—but I could not imagine where I could get the idea from, if I had not seen it. And yet it is starting to bother me now that there is nothing in the autopsy about it.* [36, pp. 52–53]

He added:

> *At this point, I am confused why it sticks in my mind so strongly that there was this photograph, yet nobody else recalls it, and it is apparently not in any report.* [36, p. 53]

Knudsen's uncertainty and confusion indicate that he was not the photographer during the pre-autopsy when this event occurred. If he had photographed probes through the president's body, it is unlikely that he would have expressed doubt that he had, in fact, processed such film.

When asked whether he was aware that there were autopsy X-rays, Mr. Knudsen replied, "No, I do not know if any were ever taken." [36, p. 29] Accordingly, we conclude that Knudsen was not present during the official autopsy since Messrs. Stringer and Riebe—the official photographers at the autopsy—knew that X-rays had been taken [27, p. 191; 9. p. 33] and, as already mentioned, Dr. Finck requested a "whole-body X-ray survey" after his arrival at 8:30 PM [33, pp. 70, 76] . If Knudsen was in the autopsy room at some point—which we believe he was—then he was there after the official autopsy was concluded. And if he took photographs of the body—as claimed by members of his family [37, p. 4]—he did so during the reconstruction phase, thinking that he was participating in the autopsy.

A similar scenario has been suggested by Doug Horne [32, pp. 270, 593 n4, 913].

5.5. Summary

The only photographer claiming to have been continuously in the Bethesda morgue, from about 6:15 PM on 11/22/63 until the completion of the autopsy, was John Stringer. The available evidence indicates that not only did he take photographs during the official autopsy on President Kennedy's body, he also took photographs at a pre-autopsy, during which the wounds were altered.

6. Chain-of-Custody of the Casket/Body

We believe that we have established beyond a reasonable doubt that the president's body was removed from the ceremonial bronze casket into which it had been placed at Parkland Memorial Hospital prior to arrival of the bronze casket at the NNMC, Bethesda. [Section 2.] When was it removed?

6.1. Parkland Memorial Hospital to Love Field

After the president had been declared deceased at Parkland, his body was placed into a bronze ornamental casket supplied by the O'Neal funeral home for the drive by hearse to Love Field, where Air Force One was awaiting. Mrs. Kennedy was present in the hearse, with others, for this high-speed non-stop trip. [38, pp. 307–308] Upon arrival at the airport, the casket was placed on board Air Force One in the tail section and secured in place for the flight to Andrews Air Force Base.

6.2. Love Field to Andrews Air Force Base

Since the president's body arrived at the morgue in a shipping casket before the arrival of the bronze casket, it follows that the bronze casket was empty as it was taken off Air Force One at Andrews Air Force Base. Therefore, the body must have been removed from the bronze casket while on Air Force One.

6.3. LBJ's Swearing-In

The bronze casket was boarded on Air Force One at 2:18 PM CST. [39, p. 744] Mrs. Kennedy and JFK's former advisors—Kenneth O'Donnell, Larry O'Brien and Dave Powers—remained in the tail section with the casket during the flight to Andrews Air Force Base; however, they left the casket to attend LBJ's swearing-in ceremony in the mid-section of the plane, prior to take-off. LBJ was sworn in at 2:38 PM. [39, p. 744] The casket was left unattended, but for how long?

This question was first addressed by David Lifton in *Best Evidence*. He suggested that the body was removed from the bronze casket while it was unattended between 2:18 and 2:32 PM. [2, p. 677] Lifton proposed that the president's body was placed inside a body bag and hidden either in the baggage hold or in a forward galley. [2, p. 680]

In his *magnum opus, Inside the Assassination Records Review Board* [32], Doug Horne also discussed this subject and proposed that the body was removed from the bronze casket as soon as it was aboard Air Force One, even before being fixed to the deck of the aircraft, "well before the President's wife and former staff members gathered around it in flight, after takeoff, to conduct their Irish wake." Horne also suggested that the body was placed inside a body bag and stored in the forward luggage compartment, [32, p. 997] consistent with Lifton's proposal.

We made an independent study of the timeline of the activities of key individuals who left the bronze casket unattended while Air Force One was still at Love Field. The principals were: Mrs. Kennedy, Kenneth O'Donnell, Larry O'Brien and Godfrey McHugh; they accompanied the bronze casket into the tail section of Air Force One at 2:18 PM (CST). [38, pp. 352–353]

As soon as they boarded, Mr. O'Donnell asked General McHugh to go forward to the cockpit to tell the pilot to take off. [40, pp. 453, 454] After about 2 or 3 minutes the plane was still on the ground and General McHugh had not returned to the tail section. O'Donnell then went forward to discern the cause of the delay. McHugh informed him that Lyndon Johnson had given orders that he would be sworn in as president before takeoff. During this time Mrs. Kennedy left the tail section and entered the president's room. After 10 or 15 minutes Judge Sarah Hughes boarded, [40, p. 454] at about 3:30 PM. [2, p. 675]

According to the Warren Commission testimony of Larry O'Brien, shortly after boarding, there was a brief discussion between LBJ and Mrs. Kennedy, at the conclusion of which she went into the presidential compartment. O'Brien was asked by Johnson to join him and O'Donnell in the state room awaiting the swearing-in ceremony. [40, p. 470]

Now, the question is: When was the casket first left unattended? Based on the above testimonies, it appears that all four principals, Mrs. Kennedy, O'Brien, O'Donnell and McHugh left the tail section a few minutes after boarding. If we estimate 3 minutes, the time was approximately 2:21 PM. McHugh was still up front and Mrs. Kennedy, O'Brien and O'Donnell were at the mid-section of the plane awaiting the swearing-in ceremony. The latter three remained there until the ceremony was over. General McHugh apparently did not witness the ceremony. [2, p. 677], which occurred at 2:38 PM. At this time McHugh was back in the tail section. Allowing for time to have the body removed from the casket so as not to raise any suspicions from General McHugh, it is estimated the body was removed no later than 2:35 pm, which was approximately 3 minutes before the swearing-in ceremony. Therefore, we believe that the tail section of the plane was left unattended from about 2:21 to 2:35 PM, in close agreement with David Lifton's timeline of 2:18 to 2:32 PM. [2, p. 677]

What occurred when Air Force One landed at Andrews Air Force Base regarding the president's body, now out of the bronze casket? Doug Horne proposed that it was transported by helicopter to the grounds of NNMC in Bethesda, and entered the morgue at 6:35 PM, [32, p. 1003, n2] some twenty minutes before the motorcade's arrival at the front of the hospital.

6.4. On the Ground at Andrews Air Force Base

Air Force One landed at 5:58 PM. [39, p. 744] Waiting at the tail section of the plane as it landed was the honor guard under the supervision of Samuel Bird. As noted earlier, Lieutenant Bird subsequently wrote a report that described all the duties his men performed, as well as a timeline. [4] Bird and his men arrived at Andrews Air Force Base at "1730 hours," *i.e.* 5:30 PM, [4, p. 2], about a half hour before Air Force One landed. After the bronze casket, described by Bird as "solid brass," had been placed into an awaiting ambulance, he and his men left by helicopter for Bethesda, arriving at the NNMC heliport at approximately 1845 hours (6:45 PM), [4, p. 3] before the arrival of the motorcade. What occurred next is important.

After Lieutenant Bird described the arrival of his men at the heliport, his report then reads,

> *After considerable confusion as to where the President's body*
> *would be taken the joint casket team removed the casket from*
> *the ambulance at the mortuary entrance in the rear of the*
> *hospital.* [4, p. 3]

This is an eye-opening statement for a number of reasons. What did Bird mean to convey by the words "considerable confusion?" Why didn't he spell this out? How was it possible for Bird and his men to be confused as to where the president's body would be going when many high-ranking officers at the entrance of the hospital easily could have instructed them? It should have been a simple matter for the honor guard to follow the gray navy ambulance containing the bronze casket to the morgue entrance. This would have occurred except for one important detail: the bronze casket was empty. The president's body was already in the autopsy room at the time Bird and his men were at the ready to follow the gray navy ambulance to the morgue. This information had to be kept from the honor guard. Over an hour lapsed from the time Bird and his men arrived at the Bethesda Hospital to the time they performed their responsibility of carrying the bronze casket (containing the body) into the morgue at 8:00 PM. [2, p 703] What was going on in the interim?

6.5. Ambulance Chase

The honor guard, already at the entrance of the Bethesda Hospital before the motorcade arrived, had to be prevented from performing its duty, *i.e.* from immediately carrying the bronze casket into the morgue. That event had to be delayed until the president's body, now in the autopsy room for wound alterations, was placed back into the bronze casket. It would have been disastrous to the conspirators' scheme had the honor guard discovered that the bronze casket in the navy ambulance was empty. How was it accomplished?

This was elucidated by David Lifton after he spoke by phone with seven of the men who comprised the honor guard; the details are in *Best Evidence*. [2, pp. 398–422] Apparently, a "decoy" ambulance [2, pp. 402, 410] was brought into service, which Lieutenant Bird and his men followed, or attempted to follow. According to James Felder, they attempted to follow the "wrong" ambulance: after a few turns driving through the Bethesda complex, they "lost" the ambulance they were following and returned to the front of the hospital. [2, pp. 403–404] Another member of the honor guard, Navy SA Hubert Clark, indicated the ambulance they were following was speeding to the extent that they "lost it." [2, pp. 410–411] Eventually they found the "right" ambulance, but not until approximately 8:00 PM, at which time they carried the casket—now containing the president's body—into the morgue.

How did the bronze casket (empty) arrive inside the morgue without the knowledge of the honor guard?

6.6. Empty Bronze Casket: Chain of Events

We suggest that Calvin Galloway played a significant role in causing the honor guard to go on a couple of "wild goose" chases, which consumed an hour. This time was needed to complete the alterations to the body, bring the empty casket into the morgue, reunite it with the body, take it out of the morgue and place it inside the gray navy ambulance, to be "found" by the honor guard.

Shortly after the motorcade arrived, Admiral Galloway got into the driver's seat of an ambulance—the "decoy" ambulance—and took off followed by the honor guard, mistakenly thinking that this ambulance contained the bronze casket. This is the ambulance they "lost."

Evidence that Admiral Galloway, despite being commander in chief of the NNMC, assumed the role of lowly chauffeur, is provided by an article in the *Washington Post* on November 23, 1963:

> *Adm. Calvin B. Galloway, commandant of the medical center, pushed into the front seat and drove to the rear of the Hospital, where the body was taken inside.*" [2, p. 416]

Clearly, the author of the article believed that the bronze casket (and of course the president's body) was in the ambulance driven by Galloway. It would be expected that, as commandant of the medical center, Galloway knew the morgue location. And, surely, Galloway was aware that the president's body was already in the morgue. Moreover, he knew he had to keep the honor guard engaged in making futile round trips throughout the Bethesda complex until such time that all alterations of the president's wounds had been completed; the president's body had been placed back into the bronze casket; and the bronze casket had been returned to the navy ambulance.

If Galloway was driving a "decoy" ambulance, which the honor guard was chasing, who drove the navy gray ambulance containing the empty bronze casket to the morgue and at what time did this occur?

FBI Agents James Sibert and Francis O'Neill were in the third car of the motorcade as it traveled from Andrews Air Force Base to Bethesda. [25, p. 235] Upon arriving at the front entrance of the hospital, at about 6:55 PM, [39, p. 744] O'Neill said he observed Mrs. Kennedy, Bobby Kennedy, SSA Roy Kellerman and probably Dr. Burkley, the president's personal physician, exit the gray navy ambulance, which contained the ornamental bronze casket, and enter the hospital. [41, pp. 53–54] After some delay, in which the gray navy ambulance had not moved, O'Neill determined that the driver, William Greer, did not know the location of the morgue. O'Neill informed SSA Greer that he knew the way and should follow him. [41, pp. 54–55] O'Neill claimed the time they arrived at the morgue was about 7:05 PM. [41, p. 58] According to Sibert, when they arrived at the morgue entrance, he along with O'Neill, SSAs Greer and Kellerman—plus "some others"—carried the bronze casket into the anteroom, adjacent to the autopsy room. [42, pp. 44–45] The "some others" who assisted FBI Agents Sibert and O'Neill, plus SSAs Greer and Kellerman, are identified below.

An article published by the *Commercial News*, Danville, Illinois, November 20, 1988, stated that Roger Annan, a corpsman at the Bethesda Hospital, "helped carry Kennedy's body" into the morgue. It further stated that at about 7 PM, Annan and about five other corpsman, an elderly general and three Secret Servicemen carried a "1,000-pound casket" out of a navy ambulance and brought it into a "white-tiled" room, *i.e.* the anteroom adjacent to the autopsy room. [43, 44]

On March 14, 1993, Mr. Annan had a letter published in the *Commercial News* in which he stated that he with three other corpsmen plus "[f]our Secret Servicemen and one elderly Army general carried a heavy casket into the first section of the morgue area." [45]

Mr. Annan's reference to four secret servicemen likely corresponded to FBI Agents Sibert and O'Neill; and SSAs Greer and Kellerman, all of whom were in suits and indistinguishable from each other. Based on Annan's account and FBI Agent Sibert's recollection regarding the time the bronze casket (empty) was carried into the morgue anteroom, it was about 7:00 PM or a little later. More details on this subject can be found in an article recently published by the authors. [46]

7. Timeline: FBI Agents Sibert and O'Neill

The preceding discussion has established that FBI Agents Sibert and O'Neill assisted in taking the bronze casket (empty) into the anteroom of the autopsy room shortly after 7:00 PM. Surely they expected to proceed into the autopsy room with the bronze casket; on the contrary, they were kept out by being told—probably by SSA Kellerman—that "preparations for the autopsy" were on-going. They were unaware that the casket was empty and that they had to be prevented from realizing that the president's body was already in the autopsy room.

The two agents did not make note of this in their report [20] (Appendix I) and for good reason. They would have had to admit they lost vigil of the president's body/casket, a responsibility given to them by J. Edgar Hoover himself. A discussion of how this occurred follows.

7.1. At Andrews Air Force Base

After learning of the death of the president at around 3:00 PM, Sibert and O'Neill proceeded to Andrews Air Force Base to await the arrival of Air Force One carrying President Kennedy's body. [20, p. 2] Shortly before the arrival of Air Force One, Sibert spoke to the director of the Secret Service, James Rowley, informing him of their instructions from Hoover. [42, p. 39] Accordingly, Rowley placed the FBI agents in the third car of the motorcade that followed the ambulance containing the Dallas casket, from Andrews to the NNMC.

7.2. At Bethesda Hospital

The motorcade, along with Sibert and O'Neill, arrived at the front of the NNMC at 6:55 PM. [39, p. 744] Their report states that, after Mrs. Kennedy and Robert Kennedy had alighted and entered the building, the ambulance (carrying the Dallas casket) "was thereafter driven around to the rear entrance..." [20, p. 2] The word "thereafter" is a catch-all, concealing a significant delay before the navy ambulance moved to the rear. [2, p. 478] During this time, the honor guard was having difficulty "finding" the gray navy ambulance (Section 6.5.).

After the delay, caused by SSA Greer claiming that he did not know the way, Sibert and O'Neill either drove with Greer or walked [42, p. 43] to the loading dock adjacent to the morgue complex with Greer following and arrived there presumably at "approximately 7:17 PM," the time they gave to Arlen Specter for when "preparation for the autopsy" began. [47, p. 2] What happened between 7:17 and 8:15 PM, when they said that "the first incision was made"? [20, p. 4] Nothing in their report answers this question, because it's when they lost vigil of the president's body/casket.

The claim in their report that "Bureau agents (*i.e.* themselves) assisted in moving the casket to the autopsy room" [20, p. 2] is partly false. They could not have taken the casket any further than the anteroom (*i.e.* the cooler room adjacent to the autopsy room). This is supported by comments made by Mr. Sibert in retirement:

> We took [the casket] into the anteroom, like off the autopsy room, where we put it right down on the floor, the casket right down on the floor. I remember that. [25, p. 241]

The next statement in the report is:

> A tight security was immediately placed around the autopsy room by the Naval facility and the U.S. Secret Service. Bureau agents made contact with Mr. ROY KELLERMAN, the Assistant Secret Service Agent in Charge of the White House Detail, and advised him of the Bureau's interest in this matter. [20, p. 2]

These sentences convey the impression that the events—the placement of tight security and the advisement of SA Kellerman—occurred sequentially. In fact, they did not. During Sibert's deposition before the Assassination Records Review Board (ARRB), when invited to comment on this passage, he responded:

> Yes, the sequence of events is off there. Contact was made with Kellerman right before the casket even came out of the... ambulance. But the tight security, believe me, it was tight. About every 10 feet they had a guard posted in the hallway. [42, p. 57]

Therefore, when the FBI agents arrived at the loading dock with the bronze casket (empty), O'Neill introduced himself and Sibert to Kellerman, who had emerged from the door to the morgue. [32, p. 1006] They believed that an introduction was necessary, and Kellerman responded, "I know. I've already got a call from Rowley that you're going to be here." [41, p. 56]. In due course, as they entered the building with the casket, Sibert and O'Neill saw the tight security. These independent events provide a new picture of what occurred after 7:17 PM. The use of the word "advised" coupled with the comment on "tight security" has elicited erroneous conclusions for decades. The statement about tight security was merely a factual observation; it had nothing to do with their not entering the autopsy room. After all, how would the presence of FBI agents constitute a break in security? The word "advised" has been interpreted as indicating a battle of wills between the FBI agents and Kellerman, [*e.g.* 32, p. 1006] whereas a simpler explanation is that Sibert and O'Neill were merely introducing themselves to the Secret Service agent, informing him of their remit.

7.3. Explanation

What kept the FBI agents from entering the autopsy room? The answer lies in information that emerges from Sibert's and O'Neill's ARRB depositions. On their arrival at the morgue, both men said they became aware of on-going discussions about what type of autopsy—full or partial—should be performed. According to Sibert:

> *I think there were clearances—the impression that I had—that there were clearances being given by maybe Burkley, who was the President's personal physician, Admiral Burkley, or maybe Mrs. Kennedy, about a complete autopsy. And this could have been going on, talking about preparation for a complete autopsy, you're probably going to have a little different planning for a more limited type. So, this could have been part of the preparation.* [42, pp. 49–50].

Sibert's uncertainty—"I think," "the impression I had," "maybe Mrs. Kennedy," "this could have been going on," "this could have been part of the preparation"—reveals that he knew of the discussions by hearsay at best, and, we believe, sheds light on the following cryptic comment in the

FBI report that immediately precedes the description of the body being removed from the casket:

> *Arrangements were made for the performance of the autopsy*
> *by the U.S. Navy and Secret Service.* [20, p. 4]

These purported discussions provided Sibert and O'Neill with a plausible reason for a delay in the start of the autopsy, which explains their claim to Arlen Specter that "the preparation for the autopsy" began at 7:17 PM, whereas the first incision was not made until 8:15. [20, p. 4] In other words, there was no need for them to enter the autopsy room at 7:17 PM because—as far as they were aware at that stage—nothing was going on there apart, perhaps, from discussions on whether the autopsy would be complete or partial. However, at some later point, they became aware of activity in the autopsy room during their absence. Support for this thesis comes from Sibert's interview with William Law; when asked how long it was from when the body was unwrapped to when they returned to the autopsy room (supposedly after photographs and X-rays were taken), Sibert replied, "Probably close to 45 minutes, something like that":

> *Law: So, that's how long you were in the cooler room or the*
> *anteroom?*
> *Sibert: Maybe out in the hall.*
> *Law: Out in the hall?*
> *Sibert: Yes, we were excluded from where they were working.*
> *We had no idea what was going on—X-rays or nothin'.* [25,
> p. 244]

Law's interview was the first time either Sibert or O'Neill had openly admitted absence from the autopsy room for a considerable period and that they possibly had been deceived. It seems odd that, if they were asked to leave the autopsy room to allow photographs and X-rays to be taken, Sibert would complain that they had no idea what was going on. A 45-minute interval comports well with the interval between 7:17 PM, their arrival time at the morgue entrance, and 8:00 PM, when we believe they entered the autopsy room and observed the president's body for the first time. Even with this important truth expressed in his interview with Law, Sibert (and O'Neill) was guilty of what most kindly may be described as "memory merge" in their report—implying that they observed the president's body being unwrapped shortly after their arrival at the morgue, *i.e.* at 7:17 PM, when, in fact, at 7:17 PM, the body was already in the autopsy room being altered, unbeknownst to the FBI agents at the time.

Two other statements in the Sibert and O'Neill report merit discussion, because neither has received much attention. This is unfortunate since one is blatantly false. The first is:

> The President's body was removed from the casket in which it had been transported... [20, p. 4]

One might take it that Sibert and O'Neill witnessed this event. However, the wording is awkwardly in the passive tense leading us to surmise that they did not observe the president's body being removed from the Dallas casket. On this subject, a bizarre exchange occurred among Sibert, Law and Debra Conway:

> Conway: Were they in the anteroom when they unwrapped him, or when they brought him into the main—
> Sibert: I couldn't say for sure.
>
> ...
>
> Law: ...[Y]ou don't remember whether they took the body out at that point—
> Sibert: I would think, I don't know, this is just reasoning, but they had corpsmen that were carrying, you know, lifting him out of the casket onto the autopsy table and I can't—because I was talking with O'Neill. When I saw what we were up against there, I said, "We've got to get the names of everybody in this autopsy room..." [25, pp. 242–243]

Apparently, Mr. Sibert had better recollection of his concern over who else was in the autopsy room than of first seeing the body of his brutally murdered president. Moreover, in his ARRB deposition, Sibert claimed no recollection of the honor guard bringing in the Dallas casket. [42, p. 54] In O'Neill's ARRB deposition, he said that, due to vague recollection, he would have to guess as to which military branch the honor guard came from. [41, p. 58] In fact, the honor guard, whom Sibert and O'Neill had seen at Andrews AFB (Figure 1), was composed of all five services. It seems unlikely that O'Neill—who served in the US Air Force in World War II— would not have taken mental note of the servicemen in dress uniforms. Of course, any mention in their report of the honor guard would have begged awkward questions of why the Dallas casket was brought into the morgue twice. Either Sibert and O'Neill were somehow manipulated so as not to see the honor guard carrying the casket or they feigned faulty memory. (We view the former possibility as the more likely.)

The second statement meriting discussion is in the next paragraph:

> *Upon completion of X-Rays and photographs, the first incision was made at 8:15 p.m.* [20, p. 4]

This statement is questionable for two reasons. X-rays and photographs were taken throughout the autopsy, which was completed at around 11:00 PM. [32, p. 1010] In any case, it is intuitively obvious that the taking of X-rays and photographs could not have been completed within 15 minutes of the beginning of the autopsy. [32, p. 1008] Furthermore, after his arrival at 8:30 PM prosector Pierre Finck ordered full-body X-rays. We suggest that if Sibert and O'Neill first entered the autopsy room shortly after 8:00 PM, it was after the honor guard had delivered the Dallas casket, the second time that this casket had been brought in.

One more point should be made. We suggest also that once the FBI agents entered the autopsy room at some time after 8:00 PM, they did not then exit for the taking of X-rays and photographs as stated in their report. [20, p. 4] There would have been no need to clear the autopsy room at this point since all of the illicit alterations of the president's body had been completed and nothing needed to be hidden from the agents.

7.4. Conclusion

Why did FBI Agents Sibert and O'Neill produce a narrative to convey the impression that they were absent from the morgue for only 15 minutes? We suggest that their objective was to reassure their superiors that—for reasons beyond their control—the body was out of their sight for just 15 minutes after it had been removed from the Dallas casket and was on the autopsy table. Thus, they would be excused for a minor infraction in meeting their responsibility to maintain an unbroken chain-of-custody of the president's body. They needed to hide the fact that they had lost contact with it for about 45 minutes, 7:17 to after 8:00 PM.

8. Timeline: Dealey Plaza to the Bethesda Morgue

In view of the fact that many events, as well as their associated times have been discussed, it might be helpful at this point to provide a listing.

1:30 PM EST	President Kennedy is shot.
2:00 PM	President Kennedy is pronounced dead at Parkland Memorial Hospital.
3:04 PM	The body leaves hospital in a bronze, ceremonial casket.
3:18 PM	The casket is placed aboard Air Force One (AF-1) at Love Field.
3:38 PM	Lyndon Johnson is sworn in as president. During this time, the body is removed from bronze casket and hidden on AF-1.
3:47 PM	AF-1 is airborne.
6:00 PM	AF-1 arrives at Andrews Air Force Base.
6:10 PM	The bronze casket (empty) placed into a navy ambulance which departs for the National Naval Medical Center (NNMC), Bethesda. Jacqueline and Robert Kennedy ride in the ambulance which is part of a motorcade.
6:35 PM	Roger Boyajian witnesses a casket being taken into the morgue.
~6:45 PM	Dennis David and a detail of sailors off-load a shipping casket from a black hearse and take it into the anteroom adjacent to the autopsy room. (Autopsy photographer Floyd Riebe, X-ray technicians Edward Reed and Jerrol Custer, and medical technician Paul O'Connor witness arrival of the shipping casket; the body is in a body bag.)
6:50 PM	A joint-service casket team (honor guard) arrives at Bethesda Hospital.
6:55 PM	The motorcade arrives at the front entrance of Bethesda Naval Hospital (part of the NNMC complex); Mrs. Kennedy and entourage enter the building.

7:05 PM	The honor guard follows a decoy ambulance and gets lost several times on the grounds of the NNMC.
7:10 PM*	The ambulance—containing the bronze casket, without the body—is driven to the loading dock at the rear of the hospital; the casket is off-loaded and taken into the anteroom adjacent to the autopsy room by Secret Service agents, FBI agents, and hospital corpsman Roger Annan and his colleagues.
8:00 PM*	The honor guard "finds" the navy ambulance with the bronze casket (containing the body) and takes it into morgue.
8:15 PM	The Y-incision is made and the official autopsy begins.

*FBI Agents Sibert and O'Neill lost contact with the bronze casket during this timeframe.

9. The Warren Commission, the House Select Committee on Assassinations (HSCA) and the Assassination Records Review Board (ARRB): Investigations of the JFK Assassination

There follow discussions and assessments of the three agencies that investigated the assassination of President Kennedy and their findings. It will be apparent that, in spite of limited resources as well as a restricted mandate, the work of the ARRB was the only one that allowed the truth to emerge about how and why JFK was murdered. The key work performed by the ARRB was due to the efforts of Douglas Horne, chief analyst for military records. How he came to the ARRB in this capacity is described in his book *Inside the Assassination Records Review Board*. [32, pp. liii–lxxiii]

9.1. The Warren Commission and their Report

The Warren Commission (1963–1964) was a political body founded on the premise that there had been no conspiracy, that Lee Harvey Oswald was the lone assassin. In the *Warren Commission Report,* Oswald was tried and convicted, which was easy to do since he had already been murdered. The Commission's findings of Oswald's guilt were helped considerably by the work of the late Arlen Specter, whose role, as assistant counsel, was to "handle" the facts to support the Commission's foregone conclusion.

9.1.1. Introduction

On November 25, 1963, the day President Kennedy was interred at Arlington Cemetery—also the day after Oswald was killed by Jack Ruby—a memorandum by Nicholas Katzenbach, deputy attorney general, was sent to Press Secretary Bill Moyers, outlining how the investigation of the president's assassination was to proceed (Figure 13).

The first two paragraphs contain words that are chilling:

- "The public must be satisfied that Oswald was the assassin..."

- "Speculation about Oswald's motivation ought to be cut off."

This memorandum, which omitted any reference to seeking the truth about who killed the president and why he was murdered, established the mandate for the Warren Commission. It had the effect of burying, for decades, the truth about how President Kennedy was assassinated. There should be no doubt that the memorandum had the complete approval of President Johnson.

November 25, 1963

MEMORANDUM FOR MR. MOYERS

It is important that all of the facts surrounding President Kennedy's Assassination be made public in a way which will satisfy people in the United States and abroad that all the facts have been told and that a statement to this effect be made now.

1. The public must be satisfied that Oswald was the assassin; that he did not have confederates who are still at large; and that the evidence was such that he would have been convicted at trial.

2. Speculation about Oswald's motivation ought to be cut off, and we should have some basis for rebutting thought that this was a Communist conspiracy or (as the Iron Curtain press is saying) a right-wing conspiracy to blame it on the Communists. Unfortunately the facts on Oswald seem about too pat—too obvious (Marxist, Cuba, Russian wife, etc.). The Dallas police have put out statements on the Communist conspiracy theory, and it was they who were in charge when he was shot and thus silenced.

3. The matter has been handled thus far with neither dignity nor conviction. Facts have been mixed with rumour and speculation. We can scarcely let the world see us totally in the image of the Dallas police when our President is murdered.

I think this objective may be satisfied by making public as soon as possible a complete and thorough FBI report on Oswald and the assassination. This may run into the difficulty of pointing to inconsistencies between this report and statements by Dallas police officials. But the reputation of the Bureau is such that it may do the whole job.

Figure 13. The Katzenbach memorandum.

It is notable that Johnson did not have the attorney general sign this, which would have been the normal step to take. He circumvented Robert Kennedy with the foreknowledge that his attorney general would have resisted signing such a document.

In the context of the Katzenbach memo, it should not be difficult to understand why the Warren Commission was not truly an investigative body, in spite of the external appearance. Having Earl Warren the chief justice of the United States Supreme Court as the chairperson gave the Commission supreme legitimacy. Only after examining other factors in more detail, like the make-up of its members, how it was structured and the work it produced does its luster begin to tarnish.

The Commission comprised seven members. In addition to Chairman Earl Warren, there were Senator Richard Russell, Senator John Cooper, Congressman Hale Boggs, Congressman Gerald Ford, former CIA Director Allen Dulles, and John J. McCloy, chairman of the Ford Foundation. All members were hand-picked by President Johnson, had been closely connected with the United States government and, as such, would not have been permitted to serve on a jury in a trial of Lee Harvey Oswald. None had any experience in the medical field or in wound ballistics.

9.1.2. Background

Most of the work was done by a staff of fifteen lawyers, headed by General Counsel J. Lee Rankin, likewise with no experience in the medical field or wound ballistics. The Commission's work was divided into six areas.

Area I involved determining the "basic facts of the assassination." The head counsel was Francis W.H. Adams, a former New York City police commissioner. However, since Adams was heavily involved with activities of his law firm, virtually all the major work in this area was done by Adams' assistant, Arlen Specter. The rest of the Commission staff worked on: Area II, concerned with establishing the identity of the assassin; Area III, devoted to investigating Oswald's background; Area IV, concerned with Oswald's possible connection to a conspiracy and his movements outside the country; Area V, which dealt with Oswald's death and prior connection to Jack Ruby; and Area VI studied presidential protection in general. Of these six areas, four were focused on Oswald in keeping with the tone set forth in the Katzenbach memorandum. On the basis of how the Commission's areas of interest were structured, Specter must have realized what his sole purpose was even before he began his work. As an aside, approximately fifty percent of the 888 pages of the *Warren Commission Report* are devoted to Oswald.

9.1.3. Key eyewitnesses not called

In addition to selecting what witnesses were to appear for questioning, the Warren Commission staff evaluated reports written by government agencies, chiefly the FBI and Secret Service. From such reports, the staff lawyers decided what witnesses would be questioned informally and who would be brought before the Commission to testify under oath. No independent investigators were hired by the Commission. The staff lawyers relied solely on the FBI, CIA and Secret Service reports provided to them by the agencies, thus controlling the information they received. Remarkably, FBI Agents James Sibert and Francis O'Neill—eyewitnesses to the autopsy and to statements made by Dr. Humes—who had written a report about their observations,[20] and who had been interviewed personally by Specter, [47] *were not* called to testify before the Commission. None of the medical technicians, X-ray technicians or the photographers at the autopsy were called to testify. Admiral Burkley, the only medical person who was present in trauma room one at Parkland Hospital as well as at the autopsy was not called to testify. This was a critical omission. Had Dr. Burkley testified truthfully under oath, he would have confirmed the observations of the president's wounds at Parkland and (if asked) the differences in those wounds seen at the official autopsy in Bethesda.

Analysis by JFK researcher and author Walt Brown has revealed that the commissioners did little work [48] and largely failed to meet their responsibilities. Brown asserts that:

> ...the Commissioners came and went from the 'investigation
> of the century' as if it were the Friday night poker game and
> quarters were on the table. [48]

Many of their questions were perfunctory and revealed their ignorance of the subject. In many cases, commissioners failed to ask a single question of witnesses being deposed.

Almost 500 witnesses testified to the Warren Commission. Of these, only 93 did so in the presence of any of the seven members. Earl Warren was "present" for all 93 witnesses; Richard Russell was "present" for only six witnesses. And even this does not convey the entire story. Many who were assigned as "present" at depositions left early or came well after witnesses had been deposed. [48]

9.1.4. The Warren Commission's findings: Examples

Of all the eyewitnesses deposed by the Warren Commission, the three pathologists at the Bethesda autopsy, James Humes, J. Thorton Boswell and Pierre Finck, should have been considered the most important. Based on how each was questioned (or not, in the case of Dr. Boswell[8]), the commissioners felt otherwise, since they ignored important aspects of the evidence that the pathologists provided. A few examples follow.

9.1.4.1. Humes' deposition

Dr. Humes' deposition to the Warren Commission occurred with Arlen Specter asking most of the questions. An unusual mutual deference between Humes and Specter prevailed throughout Humes' deposition.

When asked the start of the autopsy, Dr. Humes replied,

> *The president's body was received at 25 minutes before 8, and the autopsy began at approximately 8 PM on that evening. You must include the fact that certain X-rays and other examinations were made before the actual beginning of the routine type autopsy examination.* [14, p. 349]

This reply was false. Dr. Humes received the body about one hour earlier than he claimed, at 6:35/6:45 PM, when the shipping casket arrived. [5, p. 3; 6, p. 5] Since he was under oath, Humes committed perjury. Surely, Specter knew this and yet did not ask a follow-up question. In fact, he had a good reason not to; it might have raised issues he did not want to pursue.

When asked about the skull X-rays, Dr. Humes provided this reply:

---

[8]   Boswell was asked fourteen questions. The upshot of his responses was, "I have witnessed the testimony of Dr. Humes and precisely agree with everything he has said."

> *In further evaluating this head wound...These had disclosed*
> *to us multiple minute fragments of radio opaque material*
> *traversing a line from the wound in the occiput* (rear of the
> skull) *to just above the right eye..."* [14, p. 353]

The right-lateral skull X-ray does not depict such a line of fragments
located according to Dr. Humes' description. There is a line of fragments,
but it is higher than where Humes said it was (Figure 14).

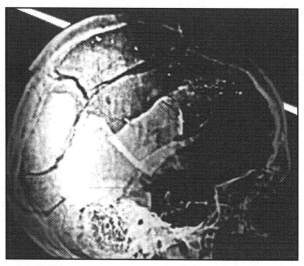

Figure 14. Right lateral autopsy X-ray showing the line of fragments.

During a discussion of the head wound, Allen Dulles asked,

> *Am I correct in assuming...that this (head) wound is entirely*
> *inconsistent with a wound that might have been administered*
> *if the shot were fired from in front or the side of the President:*
> *it had to be fired from behind the President?"* [14, p. 360]

Dr. Humes replied:

> *Scientifically sir, it is impossible for it to have been fired from*
> *other than behind. or to have exited from other than behind.*
> [14, p. 360]

This response should have elicited at least a few questions, but it did not.
What was Humes saying? Certainly, he was not implying that a bullet had

entered the rear of the president's head, performed a U-turn, and exited the rear. The only sense that can be made of this statement is that there were two bullets, one fired from the front and one from the rear. Humes appeared to be telling Specter that there were at least two shooters!

In discussing the location of the back wound, Humes added that,

> *Attempts to probe in the vicinity of this wound were unsuccessful without fear of making a false passage...We were unable, however, to take probes and have them satisfactorily fall through any definite path at this point.* [14, p. 361]

Dr. Humes was nebulous here as to whether he probed the wound and found no path or he did not probe the wound. In either case, Humes had no evidence to support his statement in the autopsy report indicating that the back wound was aligned with the throat wound:

> *The...missile entered the right superior posterior thorax...and made its exit through the anterior surface of the neck.* [3, p. 543]

Figure 15. Commission Exhibit 385.

Humes was asked several questions on how he determined that the tracheotomy site was an exit point of a bullet that supposedly caused all of Governor Connally's wounds, *i.e.* the single-bullet theory.

> Mr. McCLOY. *Quite apart from the President's clothing...you, I believe, indicated that the flight of the bullet was from the back, from above and behind. It took roughly the line which is shown on your Exhibit 385* (Figure 15).
>
> Commander HUMES. *Yes, sir.*
>
> Mr. McCLOY. *I am not clear what induced you to come to that conclusion if you couldn't find the actual exit wound by reason of the tracheotomy.*
>
> Commander HUMES. *The report which we have submitted, sir, represents our thinking within the 24–48 hours of the death of the President, all facts taken into account of the situation.*
>
> *The wound in the anterior position of the lower neck is physically lower than the point of entrance posteriorly, sir.* [14, p. 368]

McCloy should have reminded Humes that he first indicated the back wound was below the shoulders and was caused by a bullet that entered the back in a downward trajectory at an angle of 45 to 60 degrees. [20, p. 4] Humes later revised the location of the back wound to be just above the top of the scapula, making it possible to be aligned with the throat wound. He should have been asked about that also. But the point is, the throat wound was not transected and the back wound was not shown to have a path in alignment with the throat wound, of which the commissioners should have been aware. Humes merely stated that the neck wound was lower than the back wound, and, apparently, that made it so—another lie under oath.

Figure 16. Commission Exhibit 393 (arrow added).

During a discussion of the bullet holes found in the president's suit jacket, tie and shirt, the following exchange took place. When shown CE 393 (Figure 16), depicting a bullet hole in the president's jacket, Humes agreed that it was "6 inches below the top of the coat collar and 2 inches to the right of the middle seam of the coat." [14, p. 365] Humes said the same about the hole in the shirt (Figure 17). [14, p. 365] Specter then asked how well did the holes in the coat and shirt line up with the throat wound, to which Humes replied, "We believe that they conform quite well." [14, pp. 365–366] Since Humes and Specter knew that the bullet holes in the coat and shirt did not line up with the throat wound, some finesse was required of Mr. Specter. His next question was the non-sequitur of the week:

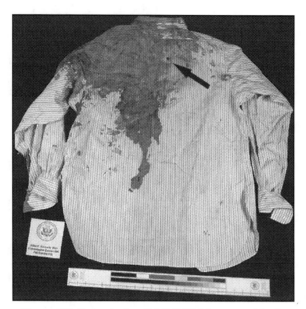

Figure 17. Commission Exhibit 394 (arrow added).

Mr. SPECTER. As to the muscular status of the President, what was it?

Commander HUMES. The President was extremely well developed...with a very well-developed set of muscles in his thoraco and shoulder girdle.

Mr. SPECTER. What effect would that have on the positioning of the shirt and coat with respect to the position of the neck in and about the seam?

Commander HUMES. I believe this would have a tendency to push the portions of the coat which show the defects here somewhat higher on the back of the President than on a man of less muscular development. [14, p. 366]

It is inconceivable that the president's muscular frame or any movement he made prior to being shot in the back would have elevated his suit jacket and shirt to the level of the neck such that the holes shown here would align with the hole in the throat. In any case, the critical issue is not the locations of the holes in the jacket and shirt, but the locations of the wounds on the body. The defect in the back (Figure 11) appears to have been at least 3 inches lower than the throat wound (Figure 3). Specter's attempt to resuscitate Humes here was ludicrous.

Dr. Humes finished his testimony on the clothing by describing his observations relating to the president's tie:

> *Situated on the left anterior aspect of this knotted portion of the tie at a point approximately corresponding with the defects noted previously in the two layers of the shirt is a superficial tear of the outer layer only of the fabric of this tie which, I believe, could have been caused by a <u>glancing</u> blow to this portion of the tie by a missile.* (emphasis added) [14, pp. 366–367]

This was nonsensical testimony. Humes referred to the "left anterior aspect" of a tie as if it were a bone! The "defects" Humes referred to in the president's shirt and tie were not caused by a bullet. They resulted from cuts made by a nurse at Parkland Hospital to quickly remove the tie. [3, p. 92]

9.1.4.2. Boswell's deposition

Dr. Boswell's deposition to the Warren Commission took place on the same day as Dr. Humes. In fact, Boswell was present to hear all of Humes' testimony. In this extraordinary deposition, consisting of one page, Boswell was asked but one essential question: "Do you have anything that you would like to add by way of elaboration to that which Doctor Humes has testified?" He replied, "None, I believe." [14, p. 377] He was not asked about any of his observations, especially in regard to the details written on his face sheet (Figure 7). If one had any doubt as to where this Commission was headed, Boswell's "testimony" made it quite clear.

9.1.4.3. Finck's deposition

Pierre Finck, the third pathologist at the official autopsy, testified to the Warren Commission on the same day as Humes and Boswell. He also was present when Humes testified. He was more experienced in forensic pathology, but not in dealing with bullet wounds. As chief of the Wound Ballistics Pathology Branch of the Armed Forces Institute of Pathology (AFIP), he had been involved in almost 400 cases, including plane crashes and other accidents.

After Dr. Finck had described his background, he gave a brief tutorial on how bullet-exit wounds are differentiated from bullet-entrance wounds; beveling of the bone in the outer aspect constitutes an exit; beveling on the inner aspect constitutes an entrance, and, in general, exit wounds are larger than entrance wounds. [14, pp. 379–380]

When asked by Specter whether he had heard "the whole of Doctor Humes' testimony," he replied, "Yes, I did." When asked if he wanted to add or modify what Humes had said, he replied, "No." [14, p. 381]

During this part of the questioning, Finck was a compliant witness, providing answers that Specter wanted to hear. However, when he was asked whether the "magic" bullet, CE 399 (Figure 18), could have exited the president's body and subsequently cause all of Governor Connally's wounds, he replied,

> *No, for the reason that there are too many fragments described in that wrist.* [14, p. 382]

This was not the answer Specter wanted to hear; however, Finck was being truthful because the loss in weight of bullet CE 399 (Figure 18)—found on a stretcher at Parkland (see below, this Section)—was much less than the weight of fragments recovered from Connally's wrist.

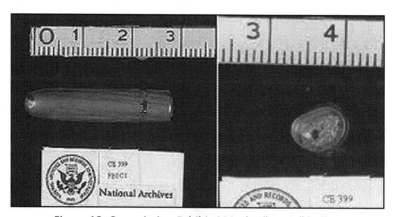

Figure 18. Commission Exhibit 399, the "magic" bullet.

Robert Shaw, one of the physicians who treated Governor Connally, also expressed doubt that bullet CE 399 could have caused all the wounds sustained by Connally because the weight of the fragments in his body far exceeded the loss in weight of the bullet. [49, pp. 113, 114]

Of more importance is the probability that bullet CE 399 did not cause *any* of the wounds sustained by Governor Connally. According to Dr. Shaw, the governor's back wound was in the form of a long, vertical, oval (CE 679) (Figure 19). Based on the single-bullet theory, before striking the governor in the back, bullet CE 399 exited the president's throat. The throat wound, according to the doctors at Parkland was in the form of a small, round hole, *e.g.* Dr. Perry described it as "approximately 5 mm in diameter." [29, p. 372] A bullet thus exiting the throat was not tumbling, and on striking Connally's back should have produced a round, not elongated, entry wound. Therefore, the governor's back wound was, very likely, caused by a bullet unconnected to any of the president's wounds.

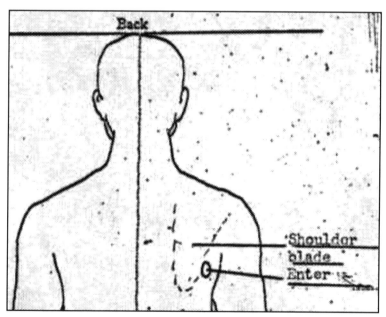

Figure 19. Part of Commission Exhibit 679, a body diagram marked by Robert Shaw, illustrating the elongated entry wound in John Connally's back.

At the end of a brief deposition, Dr. Finck was asked by Gerald Ford whether there had been any disagreements among the pathologists during the autopsy. Finck replied, "No, sir." He indicated there had been complete unanimity on what was observed and reported. [14, p. 383]

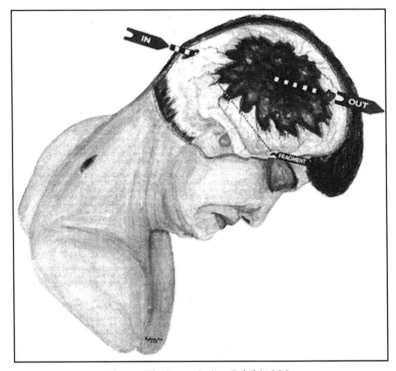

Figure 20. Commission Exhibit 388.

The last question to Finck, also from Ford, was, "Do these two wounds (as depicted in CE 385 (Figure 15) and CE 388 (Figure 20) represent the same or a different kind of bullet?" Dr. Finck answered:

> *Due to the difference in the nature of the tissue, differences in the nature of the target, it is perfectly possible that these two wounds came from the same type of bullet, that one hit bony structures and the other did not, and that explains the differences between the patterns of these two wounds." [14, p. 383]*

Representative Ford added, "Why one fragmented and one did not?" to which Finck replied, "Yes." Could it be that Ford was wondering why the bullet that hit the president's head fragmented whereas the bullet that supposedly hit Connally's rib and wrist did not?

Dr. Finck's last testimony was without merit and simply false in spite of Specter having established his opinions as bearing the imprimatur of the science of forensic pathology. The operative report on Governor Connally, written by Dr. Shaw, [3, p. 531] states that a 10-cm section of the right fifth rib was shattered. Finck must have known this as well as all the injuries sustained by the governor before he testified during the Warren Commission hearings. As such, there was no possibility of bullet CE 399 emerging from the governor's chest only slightly damaged after smashing into a rib bone and wrist. A similar bullet fired into the wrist of a cadaver (CE 856) is shown in Figure 21.

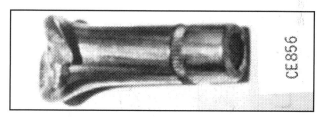

Figure 21. A 6.5-mm bullet fired into the wrist of a cadaver.

It is fitting that Dr. Finck ended the testimony from the three pathologists in a way that correlated with the conclusion of the Warren Commission Report—worthless, baseless, intentionally selective, deceitful, and containing outright lies. Humes, Boswell and Finck had important roles to play in their testimonies to the Warren Commission. Dr. Boswell was flawless because he said nothing. Drs. Humes and Finck were almost perfect, occasionally slipping when providing the truth on some details which either went unnoticed or, more likely, were intentionally ignored. The Warren Commission was given a mandate shortly after the president was assassinated: to convict Lee Harvey Oswald *in absentia*.

9.1.4.4. Autopsy notes

In Dr. Humes' handwritten autopsy notes, it is striking that the word "puncture" was crossed out wherever it was written and either omitted or replaced with something else. [50, pp. 4, 7, 8, 9] On page 4 it was crossed out; on page 7 it was crossed out and substituted with "lacerated." Other words crossed out were "tangential to the surface of the scalp." The latter reflects what was written on Boswell's face sheet: "ragged," "slanting." On page 8 "puncture" was crossed out and substituted with "occipital." It is also interesting to note that, on page 1, Dr. Humes changed his text by writing that the president fell "forward" on being shot, rather than "face downward." This change appears to have originated from orders received from Dr. Burkley since the latter's initials are in the margin. It is striking also that Dr. Humes did not write that the president's head was propelled violently backward as is depicted in the Zapruder film (Frames 313 to 324). [51] (See Appendix II.)

Therefore, salient questions are:

- Why did Dr. Humes delete all references to a "puncture" wound?
- Were these deletions made because of an order from a superior officer?
- Why wasn't he questioned about this?

9.1.4.5. Three shots from the sixth floor?

One of the more grievous deceits created by the Commission's work was how it arrived at the conclusion that the shots fired at the president came from the sixth floor of the Texas School Book Depository, thereby convicting deceased Lee Harvey Oswald as the lone assassin. This conclusion was solely based on a description of the entry and exit points of the wounds provided by Drs. Humes and Boswell from an artist's[9] drawings (Figures 15, 20). Neither the Commission nor Specter (even assuming that some members were privy to the autopsy photographs) based this conclusion on the autopsy X-rays or photographs, which were not entered as evidence in the hearings. More importantly, however, the Warren Commission completely ignored—perforce—the contemporaneous reports written by the Parkland doctors, as well as their testimony.

On page 117 of the Warren Commission Report, the conclusion of its findings was stated as:

> *Based on the evidence analyzed in this chapter, the Commission has concluded that the shots which killed President Kennedy and wounded Governor Connally were fired from the sixth-floor*

---

[9] The drawings were made by Harold Rydberg, director of medical illustration at the Bethesda Naval Medical School, on the basis of verbal descriptions from Drs. Humes and Boswell. [25, pp. 293–296] Rydberg did not see the autopsy photographs. [25, p. 295]

*window at the southeast corner of the Texas School Book
Depository Building. Two bullets probably caused all the wounds
suffered by President Kennedy and Governor Connally. Since the
preponderance of the evidence indicated that three shots were
fired, the Commission concluded that one shot probably missed
the Presidential limousine and its occupants, and that the three
shots were fired in a time period ranging from approximately
4.8 to in excess of 7 seconds.* [3, p. 117]

Note the sentence "Since the preponderance of the evidence indicated
that three shots were fired, the Commission concluded that one shot
probably missed the Presidential limousine and its occupants." This
statement is false; there is no substantial evidence that only three shots
were fired.

The conclusion that three shots were fired was based solely on the *alleged*
findings of three cartridge cases in the "sniper's nest" at the southeast
corner of the sixth floor of the Texas School Book Depository. The
conclusion that one shot "probably" missed hitting the limousine and its
occupants was based on the fact that James Tague, a bystander on Main
Street more than 200 feet downhill from the president's limousine, was
struck on the cheek by a fragment of concrete or ricochet from a bullet
that hit the curb close to where he was standing. [3, p. 116] This was the
shot the Warren Commission said "probably missed." Tague wasn't called
to testify before the Warren Commission.

9.1.4.6. Single-bullet theory
The missed shot was problematical because it forced the Commission to
explain how only two bullets caused the wounds to the president's back
and throat and all of Governor Connally's wounds. The formulation of
the single-bullet hypothesis solved the problem: all of Connally's wounds
were caused by a bullet after it had passed through the president's
neck. In order for the single-bullet theory to have merit, one important
requirement was for bullet CE 399 (Figure 18) to have been found on
Governor Connally's stretcher. This is where Arlen Specter perjured
himself. The "magic" bullet—CE 399—was found by Parkland Hospital
engineer Darrell Tomlinson who was operating an elevator between the
ground-floor (location of the ER) and the operating rooms on the upper
floors. Tomlinson told the Warren Commission how he found CE 399 and

on what stretcher [11, pp. 129–134]. In brief, he said that two stretchers (gurneys) were on the ground floor near the elevator. One of them had been placed there by him alongside another. The stretcher from the elevator was likely the one Governor Connally had been on as he was taken into the hospital. Tomlinson was badgered by Specter to say that he found the bullet on the stretcher that had been used for Connally. But having said that he had found CE 399 on the other stretcher, Mr. Tomlinson confirmed his point in no uncertain terms:

> Yes, I'm going to tell you all I can, and I'm not going to tell you something I can't lay down and sleep at night with either. [11, p. 134]

This could not be where his testimony would be allowed to end. Specter, in his usual intimidating style, forced Tomlinson to say he was not sure on which stretcher he had found the bullet. However, Tomlinson never said that bullet CE 399 was found on the elevator stretcher. Nevertheless, one week after Tomlinson's testimony, Specter assured Commissioner Dulles where the bullet had been found:

> May I say, Mr. Dulles, on that subject, I took several depositions... in the Dallas Hospital and I think we have a reasonably conclusive answer...in fact, it came from the stretcher of Governor Connally...The bullet came off of one of the two stretchers, so that, through the circumstances of the facts, it is reasonably conclusive that it came from the stretcher of Governor Connally. [29, p. 389]

This statement was false. Specter had not taken several depositions regarding where bullet CE 399 had been found and it was not a fact that it had been found on Connolly's stretcher. Had Specter been under oath, he would have been guilty of perjury.

9.1.4.7. Clarification by obfuscation
During questioning of the Parkland doctors, whenever one of them offered the opinion that the throat wound was, or may have been, an entrance wound, Specter followed up with a series of hypotheticals. He presented Charles Carrico with the following:

Permit me to add some facts which I shall ask you to assume as being true for purposes of having you express an opinion.

First of all, assume that the President was struck by a 6.5 mm. copper-jacketed bullet from a rifle having a muzzle velocity of approximately 2,000 feet per second at a time when the President was approximately 160 to 250 feet from the weapon, with the President being struck from the rear at a downward angle of approximately 45 degrees, being struck on the upper right posterior thorax just above the upper border of the scapula 14 centimeters from the tip of the right acromion process and 14 centimeters below the tip of the right mastoid process.

Assume further that the missile passed through the body of the President striking no bones, traversing the neck and sliding between the large muscles in, the posterior aspect of the President's body through a fascia channel without violating the pleural cavity, but bruising only the apex of the right pleural cavity and bruising the most apical portion of the right lung, then causing a hematoma to the right of the larynx which you have described, and creating a jagged wound in the trachea, then exiting precisely at the point where you observe the puncture wound to exist.

Now based on those facts was the appearance of the wound in your opinion consistent with being an exit wound?

Dr. CARRICO. It certainly was. It could have been under the circumstances. [29, p. 362]

And in Malcolm Perry's case:

Permit me to supply some additional facts, Dr. Perry, which I shall ask you to assume as being true for purposes of having you express an opinion.

Assume first of all that the President was struck by a 6.5 mm. copper-jacketed bullet fired from a gun having a muzzle velocity of approximately 2,000 feet per second, with the weapon being approximately 160 to 250 feet from the President, with the bullet striking him at an angle of declination of approximately 45 degrees, striking the President on the upper right posterior thorax just above the upper border of the scapula, being 14 cm. from the tip of the right acromion process and 14 cm. below the

> *tip of the right mastoid process, passing through the President's body striking no bones, traversing the neck and sliding between the large muscles in the posterior portion of the President's body through a fascia channel without violating the pleural cavity but bruising the apex of the right pleural cavity, and bruising the most apical portion of the right lung inflicting a hematoma to the right side of the larynx, which you have just described, and striking the trachea causing the injury which you described, and then exiting from the hole that you have described in the midline of the neck.*
>
> *Now, assuming those facts to be true, would the hole which you observed in the neck of the President be consistent with an exit wound under those circumstances?*
>
> *Dr. PERRY. Certainly would be consistent with an exit wound.* [29, p. 373]

Similar hypotheticals were presented to Robert McClelland [11, p. 38], Charles Baxter [11, p. 42] and Marion Jenkins [11, pp. 49–50].

It is incredible that Specter was allowed to ask such inappropriate leading questions of every Parkland doctor he deposed. Most of the doctors equivocated and gave the lawyer the answer he wanted to hear. They had little choice. On the other hand, it would have been a simple matter for each doctor to turn the tables on the lawyer by asking how a bullet hitting the president in the back at a downward angle of 45 to 60 degrees could have been in alignment with a throat wound that was located above the back wound. The lawyer's response would have been interesting.

9.1.5. Arlen Specter

In 1966, investigative reporter Gaeton Fonzi interviewed Arlen Specter and asked him what factors led him to believe that Oswald alone was Kennedy's assassin. [52] Specter's response included the following:

- witnesses saw Oswald on the sixth floor of TSBD;
- Oswald was seen carrying a package that could have been a rifle to work that day;
- there was proof that Oswald had mail-ordered a Mannlicher-Carcano rifle;
- the testimony of Oswald's wife that he owned such a rifle;

- the ballistic evidence that showed that bullet CE 399 had been fired from that rifle; and
- Oswald's flight from the scene and subsequent testimony concerning the murder of Officer Tippit.

Such evidence proved to Specter "beyond any question that Oswald was the man who pulled that trigger three times on that floor." Let's consider each of these "vital" points:

9.1.5.1. Did witnesses see Oswald on the sixth floor of the TSBD?

No eyewitnesses observed Lee Oswald on the sixth floor of the TSBD, at any time during the day of the assassination. To the contrary.

Charles Givens, a co-worker at the TSBD, was on the sixth floor during the morning. He told the FBI that he observed Oswald on the fifth floor at about 11:30 AM, at which time Oswald requested return of the elevator to that floor. Givens had gone to the first floor to prepare to have lunch. At approximately 11:50 AM, he observed Oswald reading a newspaper in the domino room which was on the first floor. [53] Moreover, Givens told the Warren Commission that Oswald always ate his lunch there. [11, p. 354]

William Shelly, another TSBD employee, told the Warren Commission that he observed Oswald on the first floor "10 or 15 minutes before 12." [40, p. 390]

Janitor Eddie Piper, told the Warren Commission that he observed Oswald "just at 12 o'clock...down on the first floor." [11, p. 383]

Secretary Carolyn Arnold told the FBI that she thought that she observed Oswald on the first floor as she was leaving the TSBD at 12:25 PM. [53]

The only person known to have been on the sixth floor immediately before the shooting was TSBD employee Bonnie Ray Williams, who ate his lunch there alone from "about 12." [29, p. 170] His estimates of how long he was there vary, but it may have taken him as long as 20 minutes to finish his sandwich, [29, p. 173] after which he went down to the fifth floor. [29, p. 171]

Based on the above, it appears implausible that Oswald was on the sixth floor of the TSBD just prior to the shooting, which occurred at 12:30 PM.

The only eyewitness who claimed he observed Oswald shooting from the sixth floor of the TSBD, was Howard Brennan. However, the Warren Commission chose not to consider Brennan's original statement about Oswald because Brennan failed to identify Oswald in a police lineup. [3, p. 145] Similarly, Ronald Fischer and Robert Edwards, were unable to identify a man they saw in the easternmost window of the fifth or sixth floor of the TSBD beyond his being 22 or 24 years old, of slender build with light-brown hair, [3, p. 146] a description that fit perhaps 10% of the population of the city of Dallas. When shown a police photograph of LHO a week after the assassination—when Oswald's face had been plastered over newspapers and in television news programs—Fischer said that it could have been the man.

9.1.5.2. Did Oswald carry to work a package that could have contained a rifle?

Two eyewitnesses claimed that Oswald had a paper bag in his possession as he left for work on the morning of November 22, 1963. Linnie Mae Randle, a neighbor, and Wesley Frazier (Randle's brother) who drove Oswald to work. Frazier said also that Oswald carried the package into the TSBD. [54, p. 797] In contrast, Randle's mother, Essie Mae Williams, who was in the kitchen with her daughter when Oswald was observed, said that Oswald was not carrying a brown bag, or anything else. Similarly, TSBD employee Jack Dougherty told the Warren Commission that he did not recall Oswald carrying anything when he entered the building for work. [11, pp. 376–377] Author/researcher John Armstrong summed up this issue as follows:

> Linnie May Randle and Wesley Frazier's testimony allowed the Warren Commission to conclude that Oswald carried a 40-inch-long Italian rifle (in the long bulky package) into the TSBD. But they never explained how the 40-inch rifle could fit into a 24- to 28-inch paper bag, nor were they able to explain why Oswald's fingerprints were not on the bag. [54, p. 797]

After Carl Day of the Dallas Police Department had covered two prints on the trigger housing with cellophane, the rifle was released to the FBI late in the evening of 11/22/63 and flown to Washington. The next morning, it was examined by Sebastian Latona, supervisor of the Latent Fingerprint Section of the FBI's Identification Division, who concluded:

> ..... the formations, the ridge formations and characteristics, were insufficient for purposes of either effecting identification or a determination that the print was [sic] not identical with the prints of people. Accordingly, my opinion simply was that the latent prints which were there were of no value. [3, p. 123]

This conclusion had to change, and it did. The story goes that, before surrendering possession of the rifle to the FBI, Lieutenant Day had "lifted" a print from the underside of the barrel, possession of which he retained until November 26. This print, mounted on a card, was received at the FBI laboratory on November 29, and identified by Latona as Oswald's right palmprint. [3, p. 123]

If this print was made by Oswald as he fired the rifle at the president, it indicates that he was left-handed because he held the barrel with his right hand. There is no evidence that the accused assassin was left-handed.

9.1.5.3. Did Oswald mail-order the Mannlicher-Carcano rifle found in the TSBD?
This is discussed further in Section 9.1.9. We agree with researcher Martha Moyer that, if Oswald had gone to trial, the rifle found on the sixth floor of the TSBD would have been exculpatory. (Section 9.1.9.)

9.1.5.4. Did Marina Oswald's testimony prove that her husband owned the rifle found in the TSBD?
Inconsistencies and contradictions in Mrs. Oswald's testimony before the Warren Commission and the HSCA have been documented by, among others, John Armstrong [54, pp. 514–520, 540, 978], particularly in relation to the rifle [54, pp. 515–517]. The text in Figure 22 provides an excellent encapsulation of how unreliable she was. In addition, the Warren Commission was never able to prove that the alleged assassin had possession of a rifle in any of his residences in Dallas, New Orleans or Irving. From March 1963 to November 22, 1963, only one witness claimed that Oswald had possession of a rifle: Marina Oswald. [54, p. 602]

MARINA

7 pag··

Marina's Testimony is so full of confusion and contradiction
that without the catalystic element of ¢¢¢¢ cross-examination it
reads like a nightmare. By her own admission Marina is a liar,
and it is her voice that tells us how intensely she disliked the
FBI and how she lied to that agency almost uniformly. When asked, for example, about the Walker note, she denied knowledge of
it, but later admitted her husband wrote it. And when asked on
December3, if she had ever witnessed her husband leaving the
house with the rifle, she replied No, but afterwards reversed this
by saying she had frequently seen Lee go in and out carrying the
rifle, once to "Lopfield" (Love Airfield) for target practice, and,
on other occasinon, to the park to shoot leaves. How, one asks,
can a man ¢¢¢ go to the park with a fifle either by day or night
and shoot leaves off the trees without being reported to the
police?

    On November 22, Marina told authorities she had never seen a
rifle WITH A TELESCOPE in Lee's possession and that the only[11]
weapon she remembered was a shotgun he had bought in Russia.
But in her appearance before the Warren Commission when comment
was made about a rifle SANS scope, she grew instantly irate and
snapped: "How is it about the telescope? HE ALWAYS HAD THE
TELESCOPE."[12] Marina's interesting statement to the FBI that Lee
"buried" the rifle in Turtle Creek on April 7th in preparation
for the Walker attack on the 10th, was ignored by the Commission;
The Commission quizzed her only about her allegation that Lee
"buried" the rifle AFTER the shooting. On the other hand, in a

Figure 22. Part of a memo from Warren Commission Staff Member
Alfredda Scobey to Commission Member Richard Russell, June
29, 1964. [54, "victors-07.jpg" on the accompanying CD]

*9.1.5.5. Is the ballistics evidence—that bullet CE 399 had been fired from
the rifle found in the TSBD—probative that Oswald alone was the assassin?*
Given the doubts underpinning the issue of whether the rifle found in the
TSBD belonged to Oswald (Sections 9.1.5.3., 9.1.5.4. and 9.1.8.) and the
fact that the bullet was found on a stretcher at Parkland Hospital, rather
than removed from President Kennedy's or Governor Connally's body, the

ballistics evidence indicates simply that, at one time, CE 399 was fired from the Mannlicher-Carcano.

9.1.5.6. What do Oswald's exit from the TSBD and testimony concerning the murder of J.D. Tippit prove?

First of all, Oswald did not flee from the scene as suggested by Specter. He was encountered on the second floor of the TSBD by Dallas Police Officer Marrion Baker at 75–90 seconds after the shooting. [3, p. 152]. Furthermore, Oswald was no more excited than anyone else would be when confronted by a police officer with his handgun drawn [54, p. 814]. Is this the characteristic of someone, having just killed the president of the United States, effecting his escape? And would an assassin leave spent cartridge cases in plain view and his weapon only partially concealed? Specter implied that Oswald murdered Officer Tippit. He did not. By the accounts of the ticket vendor and the concession attendant, [54, p. 840] Oswald was in the Texas Theater by approximately 1:10 PM, whereas Tippit was killed at a location seven blocks from the theater at about 1:10 PM. [54, p. 848].

9.1.6. Spectator Specter

If this is the evidence that Specter truly relied on to convince himself of Oswald's guilt, it's as if he were merely a spectator during the Warren Commission deliberations and forgot everything he heard.

When one considers that the original and only objective of the Warren Commission was to hide all evidence inconsistent with Oswald's guilt, it must be said that it was a huge success, ably assisted by Counselor Specter, who played the key role in burying the medical evidence that was found at Parkland Memorial Hospital—the "best evidence."

If/when the truth about the JFK assassination fully emerges and finds its way into our history books, the Warren Commission will not be judged kindly, and Arlen Specter even less so. They did their job in preventing justice from being adjudicated.

The failure of the Warren-Commission lawyers (especially Specter) to depose the autopsy photographers Stringer and Riebe, and the X-ray technicians, Custer and Reed, bordered on obstruction of justice. These men photographed and X-rayed the president's wounds during the official autopsy, albeit on an altered body. Nevertheless, had they been deposed and shown the "evidence" they were purported to have generated, the Warren Commission would have learned that many of the photographs and X-rays were missing—no longer part of the official inventory at the National Archives. And this is not all that would have been discovered. Photographs and X-rays that *are* in the current inventory were not taken by these technicians. [depositions of Reed, Riebe, Custer, and Stringer; 7, 9, 22, 27]

In addition, Dr. Humes should have been questioned by the Commission and their lawyers about the supplementary autopsy report [3, pp. 544–546] on the president's brain. This report was dated 12/6/63—as hand-written—and signed only by Humes, an oddity in itself. Had questions been asked, the commissioners would have discovered that the report did not describe the brain of John F. Kennedy. This is direct evidence of Dr. Humes' participation in the cover-up. A discussion of *SUPPLEMENTARY REPORT OF AUTOPSY NUMBER A63-272: PRESIDENT JOHN F. KENNEDY* is in Section 9.1.8.

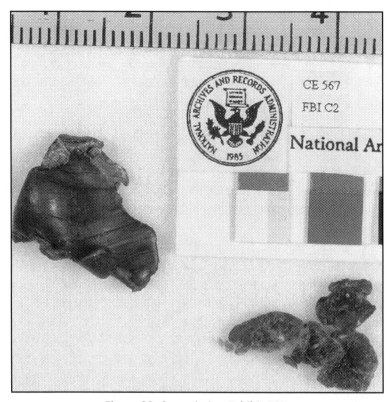

Figure 23. Commission Exhibit 567.

Undoubtedly, Arlen Specter contributed to the Commission's *CONCLUSION* in the Report because his single-bullet theory was a necessary constituent. [3, p. 117] The Commission had the audacity to present these conclusions with the knowledge that other evidence, in the commission exhibits, is totally at odds with the conclusion that only three shots had been fired. For example, on pages 76 and 77 of the Warren Commission Report, details are presented concerning two bullet fragments found in the front seat of the presidential limousine. One, a nose section (Figure 23), weighed 44.6 grains[10]; the other, a base section (Figure 24), weighed 21.0 grains. Since the total weight of these fragments (65.6 grains) is equivalent to about 40% of an intact bullet (160–161 grains), the fragments did not originate from bullet CE 399 (Figure 18), which lost very little weight even after supposedly wounding the president and Governor Connally. If they originated from a round fired at the president's limousine, but which missed the occupants, then it was the *fourth* bullet fired. On the other hand, if the fragments that matched the 6.5-mm rounds fired from a Mannlicher-Carcano rifle did not originate from a bullet fired on the day of the assassination, then they were planted as fake evidence. Neither possibility was acceptable to the Commission (or to Specter); hence, the evidence concerning the two fragments was ignored even though it was in plain view for all to see and read about. Surely Specter knew about the finding of the two large bullet fragments in the limousine: they were commission exhibits!

---

[10]   437.5 grains equal one ounce.

Figure 24. Commission Exhibit 569.

Arlen Specter maintained through the years that his single-bullet theory was correct. In 2000 he published a book [55] about the Kennedy assassination in which he maintained he was right about Oswald being the lone assassin and that bullet CE 399 produced the wound at Kennedy's throat and Connally's back, chest, wrist and thigh. Such a mindset, after decades of criticism and presentation of reams of contrary evidence, shows a proud man in total denial.

On January 4, 2012, Warren Commission critic and lawyer Vincent Salandria had lunch with Arlen Specter in Philadelphia. [56] Mr. Salandria thanked Specter for his effort during the hearings because it saved his life—a reference to avoidance of World War III with the Soviets. Salandria told Specter that, had he been given Specter's Warren Commission assignment, he (Salandria) would have done what Specter did: defend his client, the US government. In that role, Salandria would have covered up the state crime, *i.e.* the *coup d'état*. Otherwise, it might have implicated the Cubans or Soviets, with drastic consequences. But the downside—among a plethora of downsides—was that Specter did not realize that "he was no longer a citizen of a republic but rather was a subject of the globally most powerful banana republic."

Needless to say, Salandria was speaking tongue in cheek. But, did Specter get the point? It is difficult to know. Salandria ended his write-up of the luncheon with wisdom expressed by Sophocles:

> *Truly, to tell lies is not honorable; but where truth entails*
> *tremendous ruin, to speak dishonorably is pardonable.*

9.1.7. Autopsy photographs and X-rays

According to FBI Agents Sibert and O'Neill, at the conclusion of the autopsy, eleven X-rays, twenty-two 4×5-inch color exposures, eighteen 4x5-inch black and white exposures, and one roll of 120 film containing five exposures were turned over to Roy Kellerman of the Secret Service. [20, p. 6] The X-rays were developed by Jerrol Custer and Ed Reed, and examined by the pathologists during the course of the autopsy, whereas the photographic films were undeveloped when given to the Secret Service.

A record of the transfer of "items of photographic material" to Secret Service Agent Roy Kellerman—on 22 November 1963, at the US Naval Hospital morgue—was generated by John Stover, CO of the Naval Medical School and signed and dated (11-22-63) by Kellerman (Figure 25). The numbers of the film holders were later changed by Stover and initialed by him (Figure 25): the original number of eight graphic film holders for color film (each holder contains two films) was crossed out and changed to eleven, and the original number of six graphic film holders for the black and white film (each holder contains two films) was crossed out and changed to nine. These changes were initialed by Captain Stover, but not by the autopsy photographers John Stringer and Floyd Riebe, indicating that the changes were made after Stringer and Riebe had signed the document. The altered record of transfer was retyped, apparently on November 22, 1963, "certified to be a true copy" by Calvin Galloway, CO of the NNMC, and "accepted and approved" by George Burkley, physician to the president (Figure 26).

Apparently these changes were made to correspond to the twenty-two color and eighteen black and white photographs that SSA Kellerman received as indicated in the Sibert and O'Neill FBI report. [20, p. 6] However, even after the changes made by Captain Stover, the record of transfer still indicated only sixteen color and twelve black and white exposures. Even after re-typing (the version "accepted and approved" by Dr. Burkley), only the number of film holders had been changed. The number of exposed films remained the same. Thus, there is a discrepancy between what SSA Kellerman signed for (16 color; 12 BW exposures) and what he received from Stover, Stringer and Riebe, based on the FBI report (22 color; 18 BW exposures).

Therefore, the question: How many photographs were taken during the "official" autopsy? A total of forty (twenty-two color, eighteen black and white), per the FBI report, or a total of twenty eight (sixteen color, twelve black and white), based on the number of exposed film listed in the Stover memo? This very significant difference raises the possibility that neither is accurate.

The number of exposed X-rays was also changed. The original record of transfer, signed by John Ebersole and Roy Kellerman indicated a change— initialed by Dr. Ebersole—from three to six 10×12-inch X-ray films, raising the total from eleven to fourteen (Figure 27). The re-typed version (Figure 28) made the correction, but was not signed or initialed by either the radiologist, Dr. Ebersole, or the recipient, SSA Kellerman. Like the record of transfer of undeveloped photographs, it was certified to be a true copy by Stover and Galloway (Figure 28).

There are now twenty color photographs of the president's body in the National Archives, [57, pp. 7–9] as well as fourteen X-rays. [57, pp. 2–3] The Stover memo lists sixteen sheets of exposed color film (Figure 25). Therefore, there are four more color photographs at the National Archives than were taken during the "official" autopsy, which began at 8:00 PM. Seventeen X-rays are listed in the FBI report, [20, p. 5] three more than in the current inventory at the National Archives.

The Warren Commission did not pursue the reasons for those changes in the inventories of photographs and X-rays. A formal investigation of the changing inventory might have uncovered very significant findings. It should be emphasized that whether the numbers match from one document to another is not the issue. What is of more importance is whether the X-rays and photographs taken at the autopsy are the only ones in the current inventory. They are not.

Significant changes were made in the inventory in addition to changing the number of photographs and X-rays. According to Riebe and Stringer, photographs that they took at the autopsy are not part of the official inventory at the National Archives. [9, p. 41; 27, p. 126] At least two of the photographs of the president, especially of the head region, are not representative of how he appeared at Bethesda, *even after his body had been altered.*

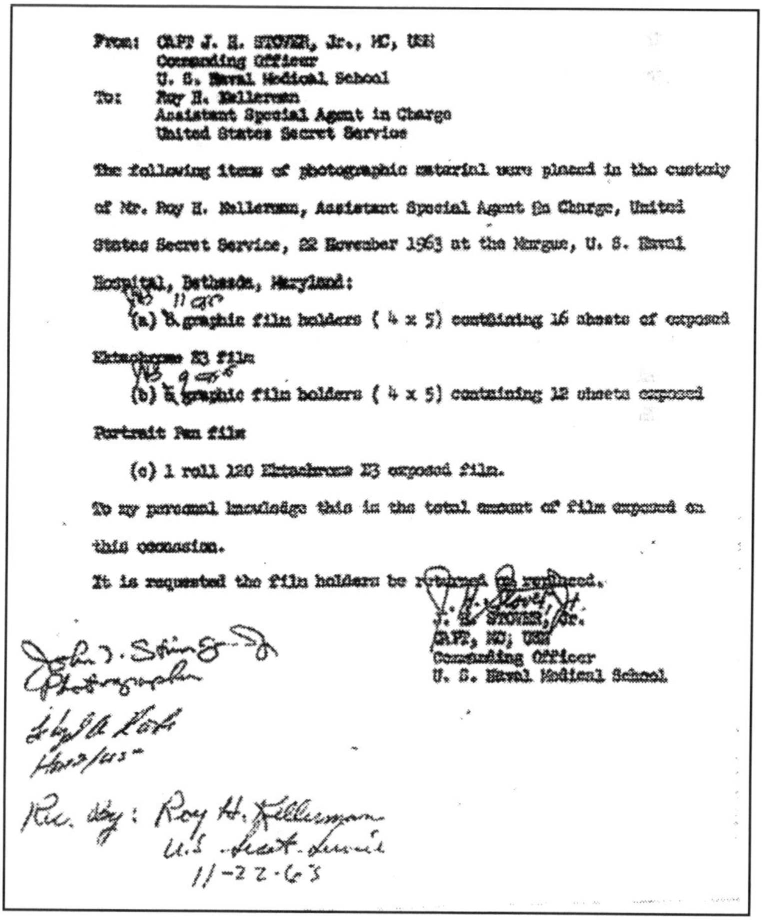

Figure 25. Record of transfer of autopsy photographs from
Captain John Stover to Secret Service Agent Roy Kellerman. [58]
(Note: The original number of film holders was changed.)

22 November 1963

From: CAPT J. H. STOVER, Jr., MC, USN
Commanding Officer
U. S. Naval Medical School
To: Roy H. Kellerman
Assistant Special Agent in Charge
United States Secret Service

The following items of photographic material were placed in the custody of Mr. Roy H. Kellerman, Assistant Special Agent in Charge, United States Secret Service, 22 November 1963 at the Morgue, U. S. Naval Hospital, Bethesda, Maryland:

(a) 11 graphic film holders (4 x 5) containing 16 sheets of exposed Ektachrome E3 film

(b) 9 graphic film holders (4 x 5) containing 12 sheets exposed Portrait Pan film

(c) 1 roll 120 Ektachrome E3 exposed film.

To my personal knowledge this is the total amount of film exposed on this occasion.

It is requested the film holders be returned or replaced.

/s/ J. H. STOVER, Jr.
J. H. STOVER, Jr.
CAPT, MC, USN
Commanding Officer
U. S. Naval Medical Schoo

's/ John T. Stringer, Jr.
Photographer

's/ Floyd A. Rabe
HM2, USN

.ec. By: Roy H. Kellerman (s/s)
U. S. Secret Service - 11-22-63

ERTIFIED TO BE A TRUE COPY:
. B. GALLOWAY
ADM, MC, USN
Commanding Officer
ational Naval Medical Center

CERTIFIED TO BE A TRUE COPY:
J. H. STOVER, JR.
CAPT, MC, USN
Commanding Officer
U. S. Naval Medical School
National Naval Medical Center

accepted & approved
G G Burkley M.D. USN
Radm Physician to the President

Figure 26. Retyped version of the record of transfer shown in Figure 25 reflecting the changes made in the original numbers of film holders. [58]

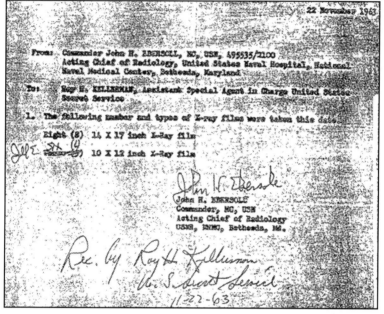

Figure 27. Record of transfer of X-rays taken at
the autopsy, from Commander John Ebersole to
Secret Service Agent Roy Kellerman. [58]
(Note: The original number of 10×12-inch film was changed.)

22 November 1963

From: Commander John H. EBERSOLE, MC, USN, 495535/2100
Acting Chief of Radiology, United States Naval Hospital, National
Naval Medical Center, Bethesda, Maryland

To: Roy H. KELLERMAN, Assistant Special Agent in Charge United States
Secret Service

1. The following number and types of X-ray films were taken this date.

Eight (8) 14 x 17 inch X-Ray film

Six (6) 10 x 12 inch X-Ray film

/s/ John H. EBERSOLE
John H. EBERSOLE
Commander, MC, USN
Acting Chief of Radiology
USNH, NNMC, Bethesda, Md.

Rec. by Roy H. Kellerman (s/s)
U. S. Secret Service
11-22-63

CERTIFIED TO BE A TRUE COPY:
C. B. GALLOWAY
RADM, MC, USN
Commanding Officer
National Naval Medical Center

CERTIFIED TO BE A TRUE COPY:
J. H. STOVER, JR.
CAPT, MC, USN
Commanding Officer
U. S. Naval Medical School
National Naval Medical Center

Figure 28. Retyped version of the record of transfer
shown in Figure 27 reflecting the changes made in
the original numbers of 10×12-inch X-rays. [58]

9.1.7.1. Visit to the National Archives

On November 1, 1966, Commanders Humes and Boswell, pathologists, Commander Ebersole, radiologist, and John Stringer, photographer, went to the National Archives in Washington, DC, to examine and catalog the X-rays and photographs purportedly taken during the autopsy. They issued a report of this inspection on November 10, 1966. [57] Author Doug Horne tabulated their findings (Figures 29, 30).

View	Description from Inventory	B & W Numbers	Color Numbers
1st	"left side of head and shoulders"	1, 2, 3, 4	29, 30, 31
2nd	"right side of head and right shoulder"	5, 6	26, 27, 28
3rd	"superior view of head"	7, 8, 9, 10	32, 33, 34, 35, 36, 37
4th	"posterior view of wound of entrance of missile high in shoulder	11, 12	38, 39
5th	"right anterior view of head and upper torso, including tracheotomy wound"	13, 14	40, 41
6th	"wound of entrance in right posterior occipital region"	15, 16	42, 43
7th	"missile wound of entrance in posterior skull, following reflection of scalp"	17, 18	44, 45
8th	"basilar view of brain"	19, 21, 22	46, 47, 48, 49
9th	"superior view of brain"	20, 23, 24, 25	50, 51, 52

Figure 29. Autopsy photographs, numbering supplied
by the November 10, 1966, inspection. [57]
(Table courtesy of Doug Horne.)

No.	Description from Inventory
1	Anterior - Posterior View of the Skull, Slightly Heat Damaged
2	Right Lateral View of the Skull, With Two Angle Lines Overdrawn on the Film (8"x10" Film)
3	Lateral View of the Skull (8"x10" Film)
4	X-Ray of 3 Fragments of Bone With the Larger Fragment Containing Metallic Fragments (8"x10" Film)
5	X-Ray of 3 Fragments of Bone With the Larger Fragment Containing Metallic Fragments (8"x10" Film)
6	X-Ray of 3 Fragments of Bone With the Larger Fragment Containing Metallic Fragments (8"x10" Film)
7	Anterior - Posterior View of the Abdomen (14"x17" Film)
8	Anterior - Posterior View of the Right Shoulder and Right Chest (14"x17" Film)
9	Anterior- Posterior View of the Chest (14"x17" Film)
10	Anterior- Posterior View of the Left Shoulder and Left Chest (14"x17" Film)
11	Anterior- Posterior View of the Abdomen and Lower Chest (14"x17" Film)
12	Anterior - Posterior View of Both Femurs including Both Knee Joints (14"x17" Film)
13	Anterior - Posterior View of the Pelvis. There is a Small Round Density of Myelogram Media Projected Over the Sacral Canal (14"x17" Film)
14	Anterior- Posterior View of Lower Pelvis, Hips, and Upper Femurs (14"x17" Film)

Figure 30. Autopsy X-rays, numbering supplied by
the November 10, 1966, inspection. [57]
(Table courtesy of Doug Horne.)

The most significant findings of the report are:

- There is a total of fourteen X-rays, per the record of transfer signed by Ebersole (Figure 27), but six X-rays are of 8×10 inches as opposed to 10×12 as originally listed.
- There are eighteen 4×5-inch black-and-white negatives of the body, which agrees with the original number listed in the FBI report, [20, p. 5] numbered 1 to 18.
- There are twenty 4×5-inch color positive transparencies of the body, two less than listed in the FBI report, numbered 26 to 45.
- There are seven 4×5-inch black and white negatives of the brain, which agrees with the supplementary autopsy report. [3, p. 545] These are numbered 19 to 25.
- There are seven 4×5-inch color transparencies of the brain, numbered 46 to 52, one more than Dr. Humes stated in the supplementary autopsy report.

The eighteen black and whites and the twenty color transparencies do not represent different "shots" of the president's body. Some of the photographs vary only slightly in the camera angle and/or magnification, likewise for the brain photographs. Seven different positions of the president's body and two different views of the brain were photographed (Figure 30).

Subsequent to the November 10, 1966, inventory report, which merely served as cataloging, Drs. Humes and Boswell re-visited the National Archives—on January 20, 1967—this time with Dr. Finck. [59] Their purpose was to link the autopsy findings with the photographic evidence.

9.1.7.2. Autopsy photographs
The seven extant autopsy photographs of the president's body are shown in Figures 31–37. The captions (see Figure 30, *Description from Inventory*) correspond to the descriptions in the November 10, 1966, inventory report prepared by Drs. Humes, Boswell and Ebersole, plus photographer Stringer: [57]

- *Autopsy photograph, View #1, left side of head and shoulder* (Figure 31)—This corresponds to photographs #1–4 (BW) and #29–31 (color) (Figure 29). What is odd about this photograph is the unreal appearance of the hair, as if a "mop" of wetted, matted hair had been placed on top of the head. The underlying hair is closely cropped, which does not appear to match the rest of the hair. The gaping incision in the neck (Section 3.1.2.) is visible at the left edge .

- *Autopsy photograph, View #2, right side of head and shoulder* (Figure 32)—This corresponds to photographs #5 and 6 (BW) and #26–28 (color) (Figure 29). The damage shown here is principally located on the top right of the head.

- *Autopsy photograph, View #3, superior view of head* (Figure 33)—This corresponds to photographs #7–10 (BW) and photographs #32–37 (color) (Figure 29). These are similar to View #2 in that the damage is concentrated on the top right side of the head.

- *Autopsy photograph, View #4, posterior view of wound of entrance of missile high in shoulder* (Figure 34)—This corresponds to photographs #11 and 12 (BW) and #38 and 39 (color) (Figure 29). Supposedly it shows an entrance wound in the upper back near the top and to the right of the ruler (per Ida Dox's illustration for the HSCA, Figure 11). The placement of the ruler is odd, having no bearing on the location of the back wound described in the autopsy report:"...14 cm. below the tip of the right mastoid process (the bony protuberance behind the ear...and 14 cm. from the tip of the right acromion process (the bony tip of the shoulder)" (Figure 9). Moreover, the "back wound" appears to be more like a blood clot. The rear section of the head is intact; neither Dr. Humes' description of the head wound in the autopsy report, [3, p. 540] nor the observations at Parkland Hospital (*e.g.* Figure 5) conform to this photograph.

- *Autopsy photograph, View #5, right anterior view of head and upper torso, including tracheotomy wound* (Figure 35)—This corresponds to photographs #13 and 14 (BW) and photographs #40 and 41 (color) (Figure 29). It shows a wide, gaping throat wound with irregular edges. The width of the wound appears to be about 7 to 8 cm, whereas at Parkland Hospital it was 2 to 3 cm and did not have irregular edges.

- *Autopsy photograph, View #6, wound of entrance in right posterior occipital region* (Figure 36)—This corresponds to photographs #15 and 16 (BW) and photographs #42 and 43 (color) (Figure 29).

Supposedly, it shows an entrance wound in the cowlick area. However, this location shows merely a red spot, not obviously a wound. In the artist's representation of this photograph (prepared for the HSCA), the spot is more prominent (Figure 36, lower). A fleshy or tissue-like white object is near the rear hairline. A large flap of skull bone is visible on the forward right side of the head, under which—according to John Stringer—"there wasn't any bone and part of the brain was gone." [27, p. 198] As in View #4, the rear of the head is intact and the hair appears to have been washed. No eyewitness, including Riebe and Stringer, recalls this. Therefore, this photograph may have been taken during reconstruction— after the autopsy had been concluded—by someone other than Riebe or Stringer, the official autopsy photographers.

- *Autopsy photograph, View #7, missile wound of entrance in posterior skull, following reflection of scalp* (Figure 37)—This corresponds to photographs #17 and 18 (BW) and photographs #44 and 45 (color) (Figure 29). Interpretation of this photograph is difficult because the orientation is unclear, *i.e.* what represents the front and back of the skull. Based on David Mantik's analysis [60, pp. 293–294] of this photograph, the following points can be made:

  - This photograph appears to be a true representation of the head wound.
  - The line AB is parallel to the sagittal suture (the junction of the left and right parietal bones, Figure 4), with A pointed toward the forehead and B pointed toward the rear of the skull. The line AB divides the skull into a left and right section.
  - The defect is located primarily in the right rear occipital region, in agreement with the location of the head wound observed by the Parkland doctors.
  - The white glistening material on the upper left of the photograph represents reflected scalp.
  - The wound appears to be blasted outward (toward the rear), consistent with a frontal shot.
  - The semi-circular notch exhibits beveling in a rearward direction, evidence of an exit wound.

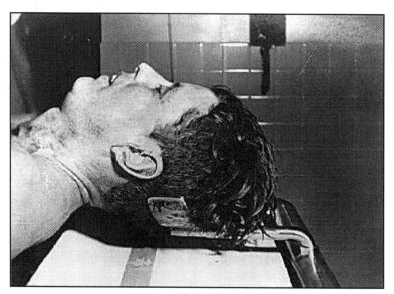

Figure 31. Autopsy photograph, View #1;
"left side of head and shoulders" (Figure 29).

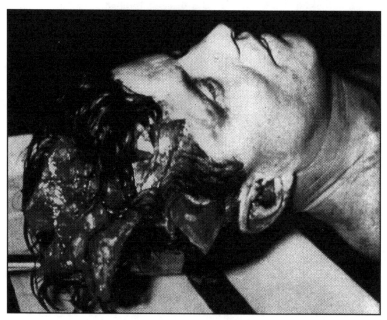

Figure 32. Autopsy photograph, View #2;
"right side of head and right shoulder" (Figure 29).

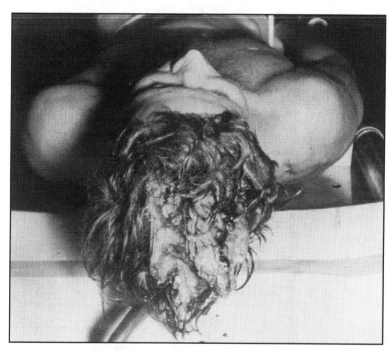

Figure 33. Autopsy photograph, View #3;
"superior view of head" (Figure 29).

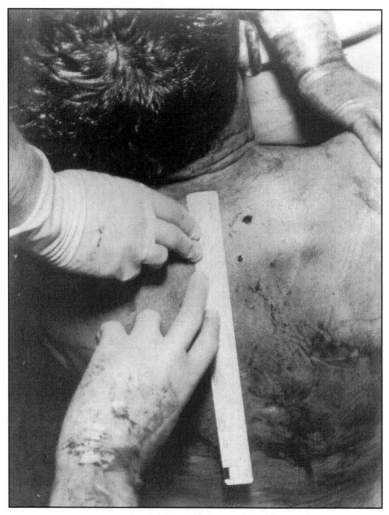

Figure 34. Autopsy photograph, View #4;
"posterior view of wound of entrance of
missile high in shoulder" (Figure 29).

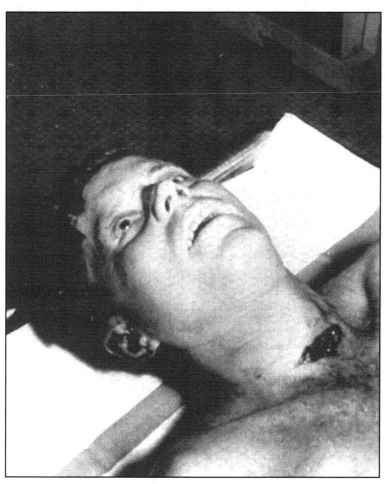

Figure 35. Autopsy photograph, View #5;
"right anterior view of head and upper torso,
including tracheotomy wound" (Figure 29).

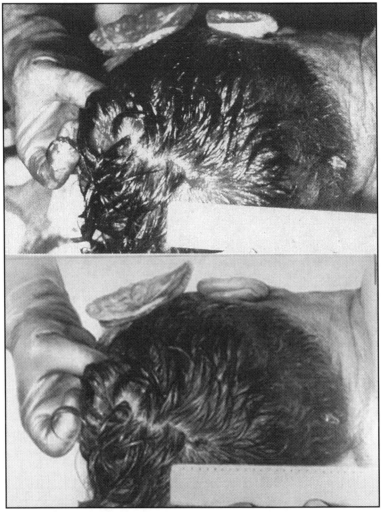

Figure 36. Autopsy photograph, View #6 (upper);
"wound of entrance in right posterior occipital region" (Figure 30).
Illustration by Ida Dox (lower, see footnote 5).

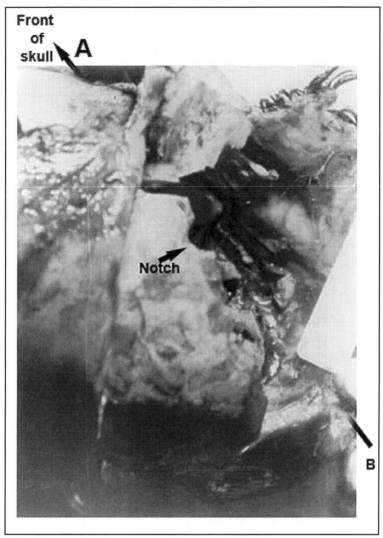

Figure 37. Autopsy photograph, View #7; "missile wound of entrance in posterior skull, following reflection of scalp" (Figure 30).

9.1.7.3. Autopsy X-rays

There are fourteen X-rays of the head and body at National Archives II. [57, pp. 2–3] This section will deal solely with the description of the anterior–posterior (A–P) and the right-lateral X-rays of the head, which are shown in Figure 38.

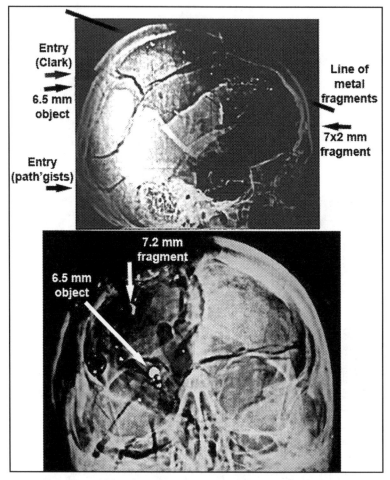

Figure 38. Lateral (top) and anterior–posterior (A–P) autopsy X-rays.

Some features are annotated on the two X-rays:

- A 6.5-mm object, quite prominent on the A–P X-ray, [60, p. 254] is located at the posterior surface of the skull, as seen in the lateral X-ray. [60, p. 250]
- A 7×2-mm. fragment, located in the frontal region, [60, p. 250 Figure 11A] was one of the fragments recovered by the pathologists during the autopsy. [3, p. 541]
- A line of metal fragments is located in the upper region of the skull.

- The point of entry of the bullet causing the head wound, as determined by the pathologists during the autopsy. [60, p. 235, see Figure 9A]
- The point of entry of the bullet causing the head wound as determined by the Clark Panel. [61]

Noteworthy is the relatively dense rear section of the skull, as seen in the lateral X-ray. This is inconsistent with the blown-out wound in the right-rear section of the head reported by the Parkland doctors. This dense region in the right rear is also at odds with the autopsy report, which described the head wound as a right parietal-temporal-occipital defect. This lateral X-ray shows a huge blown-out exit wound on the right side of the skull, above and in front of the ear.

The X-rays are consistent with the autopsy photographs in that both show the rear of the head intact. However, they are in conflict with the observations made by doctors at Parkland Hospital and during the autopsy.

The fact that these two X-rays are in concert with the autopsy photographs was to become the basis for conclusions arrived at by the Clark Panel and by the HSCA, both of whom disagreed with the reports of the Parkland doctors and with the Bethesda pathologists regarding the head wound. A short history of how this came about follows.

Recall that the Bethesda pathologists reviewed the autopsy photographs and X-rays on two occasions at the National Archives. The first was on November 1, 1966, when Drs. Humes and Boswell made the visit along with radiologist Dr. Ebersole and photographer Stringer. This was the first time they had seen the autopsy photographs. After this review—principally for the purpose of cataloging—they signed a document stating:

> The X-rays and photographs described and listed above include all the X-rays and photographs taken by us during the autopsy, and we have no reason to believe that any other photographs or X-rays were made during the autopsy. [57, p. 11]

Drs. Humes and Boswell returned to the Archives on January 20, 1967, this time with the third pathologist, Dr. Finck, who had been absent during the previous review. After a somewhat detailed description of the autopsy photographs and X-rays, the three pathologists wrote a report [59] and in the Summary section stated:

> *The photographs and X-rays corroborate our visual observations during the autopsy and conclusively support our medical opinions as set forth in the summary of our autopsy report.* [59, p. 5]

They also stated:

> *The X-ray films established that there were small metallic fragments in the head. However, careful examination at the autopsy, and the photographs and X-rays taken during the autopsy, revealed no evidence of a bullet or of a major portion of a bullet in the body of the President and revealed no evidence of any missile wounds other than those described above.* [59, p. 4]

This statement begs the question of what constitutes "a major portion." The A–P X-ray (Figure 38), shows the obvious presence of a 6.5-mm "fragment," which the pathologists chose not to discuss. Why not? Because, we contend, it was not there at the time of the autopsy.

9.1.8. Supplementary report of autopsy A63-272

Part of the *Warren Commission Report* [3, pp. 544–546] and purportedly an examination of the brain after fixation in formalin, the supplementary report contains several surprises. It is signed only by Dr. Humes and routed through Captain Stover and Admiral Galloway to "The White House Physician." The date of 12/6/63 is penciled in by Humes. The brain was recorded as weighing 1,500 g, in excess of the normal weight of 1,300–1,400 g, [62] even though observations at Bethesda indicated that a large portion of the brain was missing. Autopsy technician James Jenkins placed the brain in formalin for infusion. In a telephone conversation with David Lifton, he said, "...at least one-third of the skull was gone when Kennedy was brought in..." [2, p. 610]

The supplementary report is unusual for other reasons. In the first paragraph, reference is made to a number of lacerations:

*...a longitudinal laceration of the right hemisphere...additional
lacerations extending in various directions and for varying
distances from the main laceration.* [3, p. 544]

This description is not what would be expected from a gunshot wound.
Brain damage caused by a bullet is typically in the form of a cone of
destruction with a focus of lacerated brain tissue beneath the point of
impact and expanded damage at the exit point. If there is an exit, the
track of damage will connect the entry and the exit wounds. In contrast,
Humes described the wounds in linear back-to-front patterns that
extended deep into the head and, in one case, extended all the way from
the back to the front. As originally posed by David Lifton, could a bullet
that had fragmented produce multiple linear lacerations? [2, p. 465] In
addition, this description indicates damage more extensive than what is
described in the autopsy report. [3, p. 541] When deposed by the Warren
Commission, someone should have asked him about the supplementary
report, specifically whether a multi-lacerated brain with deep and lengthy
wounds could have resulted from a single fragmenting bullet, and, at that,
a bullet that was fully jacketed to prevent fragmentation.

In the fourth paragraph of the supplementary report, Humes states, "In
the interest of preserving the specimen (the brain) coronal sections[11] are
not made." This is highly unusual in an autopsy. Humes then indicated that
sections were taken for microscopic examination from various regions of
the lacerations, itemized as "a" through "g." [3, p. 544] Such descriptions
did not fit the usual pattern of investigation of a gunshot wound. [2, pp.
457–458]

It is important that the supplementary report (item "e") states that a
section was taken for microscope examination "from the line of transection
of the spinal cord." [3, p. 544] This indicates that the spinal cord had been
severed. But, by what or by whom? If it had been severed by a bullet or
fragment, then the brain would have been loose inside the cranium. Dr.
Humes didn't state that in the autopsy report. If Humes made the section,
why would he take a specimen from a cut that he himself had made? He

---

[11]   Coronal sections are transverse sections parallel to the coronal suture (see
Figure 8).

should have been asked about this. Unfortunately, all slides of brain tissue are missing. [2, p. 463]

On October 24, 1966, David Lifton placed a call to a neurosurgeon and read him sections of the supplementary report. After Lifton read the first paragraph describing a parasagittal (mid-line) laceration, [3, p. 544] the doctor responded, "That brain's been sectioned." [2, p. 200] And when Lifton read the section describing a tear through the left cerebral peduncle, the doctor said that this damage sounded like it had been made with a knife, not caused by a bullet. [2, p. 201] (The two cerebral peduncles are located at the underside of the brain, just above the roof of the mouth.)

For a second opinion, Lifton showed the supplementary report to a doctor at the UCLA Medical School in November, 1966, who opined that it described surgery performed prior to the autopsy. Deep lacerations in the various sections of the brain could not have resulted from a bullet. Moreover, the doctor noted that since bullet fragments were found only on the right side of the brain, what accounted for the lacerations on the left of the underside? [2, p. 251] In regard to the parasagittal laceration, a third doctor said, "Sounds like he was hit with an ax." [2, p. 466]

Clearly, the brain lesions described by Humes in the supplementary report could not have been caused by a bullet. And yet, in the FINAL SUMMARY, he said:

> *This supplementary report covers in more detail the extensive degree of cerebral trauma in this case. However, neither this portion of the examination nor the microscopic examination alter the previously submitted report or add significant details to the cause of death.* [3, p. 545]

Therefore, in spite of the fact that the observations provided in the supplementary report showed brain damage that could not have been caused by a bullet, Humes still concluded that President Kennedy had died from a single bullet to the head, as in the autopsy report.

It is important also that, in the supplementary autopsy report, [3, pp. 544–545] Humes did not mention finding metal fragments in any of the sections that were removed for microscopic examination. Had the lacerations been produced by metal fragments, such evidence should have been observed.

Doug Horne has shown beyond a reasonable doubt, in our opinion, that the damage Humes described in the supplementary autopsy report was to the president's brain, but only after he (Humes) had performed alterations on it. A second examination was made on a substitute brain, as represented in Figure 39. [32, pp. 777–844] In a nutshell:

> *The condition of the real brain was consistent with the reports of the Dallas doctors, who said President Kennedy had an exit wound in the right rear of the head, from which damaged cerebral and cerebellar tissue extruded. Allowing it to remain in evidence would have confirmed that the president was shot from the front, and would have made it impossible to sell the "cover story" to the American people.*
>
> *Removing the real brain from evidence and substituting photographs of another brain, with intact cerebellar hemispheres, and with a pattern of damage roughly consistent with a shooter from above and behind, would support the "cover story" that a lone man in a building shot a man in a car from above and behind. It also had the added benefit that it could be used to discredit the testimony and observations of the Dallas doctors.* [63, p. 308]

Horne's statement about a substituted photograph, representing someone else's brain, is supported by an official representation of the brain at the National Archives—the drawing of a superior view of the brain purported to be that of the president (Figure 39). The cerebellum is intact, in contrast to observations of the Parkland doctors of extruded cerebellar tissue. This illustration is not of the president's brain.

9.1.9. The alleged murder weapon

Another example in which the Commission ignored exculpatory evidence for Oswald was related to two of its exhibits.

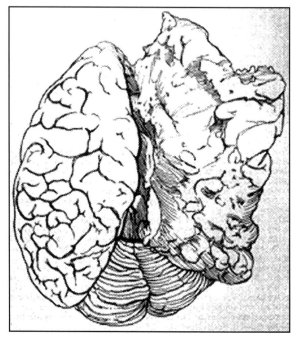

Figure 39. An illustration by Ida Dox for the HSCA, purportedly
corresponding to an autopsy photograph of the brain. [64]

Oswald was alleged to have fired three rounds at the president from
the sixth floor of the Texas School Depository Building. Shortly after,
the Dallas police found a 40-inch 6.5-mm, bolt-action rifle, S/N C2766,
with a 4× Japanese scope while searching the sixth floor [3, pp. 129, 132,
142] During their investigation of when and how Oswald obtained this
weapon, the FBI found that, on March 12, 1963, he allegedly—*i.e.* using
the alias "A. Hidell"—ordered an Italian rifle from an advertisement in the
February 1963 issue of the magazine *American Rifleman*. [65, p. 635] The
advertisement was placed by Klein's Sporting Goods in Chicago (Figure 40):

> *6.5 ITALIAN CARBINE. Only 36" overall...6-shot clip fed...C20-T750.*
> *Carbine with Brand New Good Quality 4X Scope...$19.95* [66]

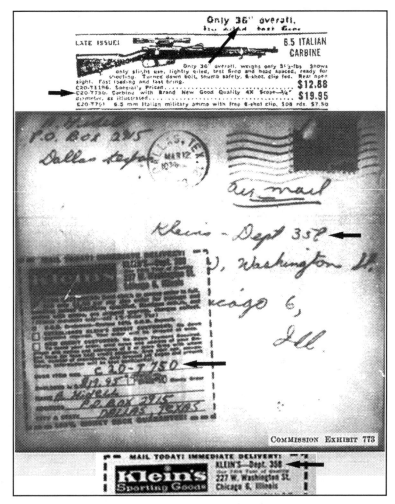

Figure 40. Top: The ad that appeared in the February 1963
issue of *American Rifleman*, for catalog number C20-T750,
a 36-inch carbine fitted with a 4× scope. [66] Middle: The
order placed by A. Hidell, mailed on March 12. [65, p. 635]
Bottom: "Dept. 358" defines the order form as clipped from
the February 1963 *American Rifleman*. [40, p. 367]

Note that Klein's Sporting Goods was advertising a 36"-long rifle, whereas
the rifle found in the Book Depository was 40" long. [3, p. 553] We agree
with a statement made by Martha Moyer in her 1996 article *ORDERING
THE RIFLE*:

> *If Oswald had lived and stood trial, I believe that an effective defense would have centered on the backyard photos in which the rifle apparently is 40 inches long. With persuasive circumstantial evidence of the delivery of a 36-inch weapon, Oswald's own argument for the alteration of the photos in order to frame him would have been strong.* [66, p. 33]

Another oddity related to the alleged murder weapon lies in the original FBI evidence sheet, Exhibit 10-13A, in which two cartridge cases—"spent rounds"—are listed as recovered from the sixth floor of the TSBD. [67, p. 112] The typed number "2" was changed to a handwritten "3." [67, p. 113] Considering that a live round was chambered in the weapon found on the sixth floor, [3, p. 79] the presumed assassin in the "sniper's nest" had restricted himself to, at most, four rounds, even though the clip held six.

Thus, the conspirators were prepared for all contingencies—lies, forgeries, altered documents, alterations of the president's wounds, intimidations— much in the realm of the expertise of organized crime, whereas, in this case, our own government was responsible.

And one further point should be made concerning Oswald allegedly shooting a Carcano rifle from the sixth floor of the TSBD. The bullet that struck President Kennedy in the head disintegrated. It broke up into fragments, some very small, as it passed through the skull bone. Such fragments are visible in the lateral X-ray (Figure 38). Bullet CE 399, purportedly fired by Oswald, did not fragment in spite of all of the damage it was claimed to have caused to the president and Governor Connally (Figure 18). How could Oswald have fired two different types of bullet from the same weapon? He didn't.

9.1.10. The case for two Oswalds

The Warren Commission was aware of Oswald impersonators, but chose to ignore the implications since they were inconvenient to creating a persuasive account of a lone assassin. [67, pp. 313–314] A comprehensively sourced, 1,000-page book on two Oswalds—*Harvey and Lee*—has been published by John Armstrong [54].

Figure 41. Lee Oswald (left) and Harvey
Oswald (right). [54, pp. 247[12], 877[13]]

The photograph on the left of Figure 41 shows "Lee" Oswald, the imposter
as discussed throughout Armstrong's book. The photograph on the right,
identified as "Harvey" Oswald shows the "real" Oswald, the alleged
assassin of President Kennedy who was murdered by Jack Ruby. Author
Armstrong's massive and detailed book provides copious proof of the
existence of two Oswalds.

9.1.10.1. Rifle-range incidents
Two eyewitnesses told the FBI that Oswald was at a target-practice
range in Dallas on September 28 and November 10, 1963. One of them
testified to the Warren Commission to that effect. [3, pp. 318–319] The
problem with these accounts is that they are in conflict with evidence
of Oswald's activities during these timeframes published in the Warren
Commission Report. The Warren Commission placed Oswald in Mexico
City on September 28. [3, pp. 734–736] And, according to the Warren
Commission Oswald was at the Paine residence from Friday November 8
through Monday November 11. [3, p. 740]

9.1.10.2. Mexico City trip
At the time Oswald was alleged to have been in Mexico City attempting
to obtain a visa from the Cuban consulate, another Oswald visited the
Odio sisters in Dallas. [67, pp. 318–327] The CIA's monitoring of the Cuban

---

12 Armstrong's reference on the accompanying CD: 59-21.
13 Armstrong's reference on the accompanying CD: NOV 22-23-01.

consulate showed that the "Oswald" there was an imposter; however, they chose not to disclose this because it would have revealed how the real Oswald was being set up as a patsy. Moreover, the Cuban consulate was bugged, which allowed the conversations between the imposter and Cuban consulate workers to be recorded by CIA stationed in Mexico City. On November 23, 1963, FBI Director Hoover informed President Johnson that the "Oswald" recorded on tape and video, did not correspond to the alleged assassin; in other words, there was an imposter in Mexico City. [67, pp. 352–353]

9.2. The House Select Committee on Assassinations and their Report

The House Select Committee on Assassinations was formed as a result of a report written by the Schweiker-Hart Subcommittee of the Senate Select Committee on Intelligence. This report expressed the view that the intelligence agencies involved with the Warren Commission's investigation had not performed credibly, giving the perception of a cover-up. On the basis of this serious view, Congress felt the need and legal right for a reinvestigation, hence the establishment of the HSCA. Critics of the Warren Commission's findings, and the public at large, were hopeful that the HSCA—particularly the forensic pathology panel—would resolve conflicting medical evidence.

9.2.1. Time wasted

The following is a summary of what transpired at the HSCA during the early months. [68, pp. 175–226]

In 1975 Congressmen Henry Gonzalez and Thomas Downing each introduced legislation to reopen the Kennedy assassination. In the bill offered by Gonzalez, the murders of Martin Luther King and Robert Kennedy were to be included, which were of interest to the Black Caucus. [68, p. 175] Downing's bill was solely on the Kennedy assassination because he had serious doubts about the conclusions in the Warren Commission Report. After more than a year, the two bills were merged, dropping the Robert Kennedy probe, and passed in September 1976. [68, p. 175]

Congressman Downing was named chairman of the HSCA. His first choice for the chief counsel and staff director was Washington attorney Bernard

Fensterwald. After objections from Congressman Gonzalez about this choice, Fensterwald withdrew. The two congressmen settled on Richard Sprague as the Committee's chief counsel. [68, p. 176]

Richard Sprague, as first assistant district attorney in Philadelphia, had been a successful prosecutor in criminal cases. In seventy cases, he had achieved sixty-nine convictions. After his selection, Sprague made it clear that he would proceed only on the condition that he had complete authority to hire his staff and perform his duty as he saw fit. He proposed two separate investigations and staff. One for the JFK assassination, one for the MLK assassination. Sprague informed Congress that he needed at least $6.5 million per year and 200 staff to do the job. In December, 1976, he asked Gaeton Fonzi to join the Committee as a staff investigator. [68, p. 177]

Sprague wasn't long on the job before he was publically criticized by some congressmen for intending to use lie detectors, voice-stress evaluators, and concealed tape recorders as investigative tools. He had never said that this was his intent and was understandably concerned about these accusations, not knowing why they had been directed at him. He was also accused of arrogance for asking such a large budget and staff. Those familiar with the bureaucracy of Washington advised him to ask for less first and then more later as the investigation proceeded. Sprague refused to play ball. [68, p. 181]

On January 2, 1977, articles in the *Philadelphia Bulletin* and *New York Times* were critical of Sprague, challenging the successful career he had established in Philadelphia. These articles provided the ammunition that some congressmen wanted: Sprague's budget proposal and the constitution of the Committee had to be reviewed, producing a lengthy delay. [68, p. 179]

On February 2, 1977, the House voted to reconstitute the Committee, temporarily. Sprague was given a much reduced staff, with salaries decreased by 40%. His first priority was to justify its existence. Under these conditions, it was almost impossible to develop new evidence. It would get worse.

From the outset, Chairman Gonzalez and Sprague did not get along. Gonzalez accused Sprague of hiring extra staff without informing him, which Sprague denied. Sprague was told that he had a $150,000 monthly budget, only to learn that he had about half of that. [68, p. 181]

Gonzalez wanted Sprague to reduce staff, which he refused to do. The chairman subsequently denied the Committee staff access to FBI files and cut off long-distance telephone calls. Within a few days, on about February 10, 1977, Sprague was fired. [68, p. 182]

Ironically, Gonzalez got himself in trouble with Congressman Richardson Preyer, head of the Kennedy Subcommittee, [68, p. 183] and was forced to resign a month after he had fired Sprague. A new chairman was chosen, Louis Stokes, a leader of the Black Caucus. [68, p. 186] The new chief counsel, G. Robert Blakey, was appointed on June 20, 1977. [68, p. 202] Nine months had been frittered away.

9.2.2. Blakey takes charge

Robert Blakey was a criminal law professor at Cornell University. He had also worked in the Justice Department under Robert Kennedy as one of the experts in the field of organized crime. [68, p. 7] Blakey's role with the HSCA was to ensure that the Mafia would be blamed for Kennedy's assassination.

During the first general staff meeting in August, 1977, Blakey told the staff that he had promised Chairman Stokes that a final report would be written by December 31, 1978; they had sixteen months to complete a "full and complete investigation." It became clear to the staff that Blakey's principal intent was to produce a report by that deadline and not investigate the assassination of President Kennedy. Blakey announced that they were not to conduct a criminal investigation and not to produce indictments.

The staff was hand-shackled from the start and, thus, doomed to fail. A committee that had at its disposal full subpoena power, access to the autopsy photographs and X-rays and the eyewitnesses at the Bethesda morgue who were not deposed by the Warren Commission, was sabotaged by the Committee chairman and chief counsel, the very people given the responsibility to find the truth. And the failure of the HSCA's investigation was made complete by the forensic pathology panel.

9.2.3. Forensic pathology panel

The panel—headed by Michael Baden, well known in the field of forensic pathology—was comprised of eight other experts in the field, including Cyril Wecht. With great anticipation, it was hoped that the panel, who deposed the three autopsy pathologists, would resolve issues underpinned by different observations of the president's wounds reported by the Parkland Hospital doctors versus the autopsy report, a subject which was not addressed by the Warren Commission. Many expected that the task of resolving the conflicts regarding the president's wounds would be straight forward because the panel—unlike the Warren Commission—had full access to the autopsy photographs and X-rays. But this was not to be. Their interviews of autopsy pathologist Dr. Humes and autopsy radiologist Dr. Ebersole provided very significant evidence that, apparently, they failed to grasp. In addition, the panel misinterpreted the extant autopsy X-rays. Examples follow.

Early in his deposition to the HSCA, Dr. Humes was asked what time the autopsy began. He responded, "...the president's body, as I recall, arrived 7:35, 7:40 in the evening..." [69, p. 324] Apparently, no one recognized that this response was in conflict with Lieutenant Bird's report, which indicated the bronze casket with the president's body was brought into the morgue at 8:00 PM. [4, p. 1]

The most significant failure of the forensic pathology panel was not to see the forgery in skull X-rays (see Figure 38). In the lateral X-ray, note the following:

- A line of metal fragments in the very top section of the skull. The notation *entry (pathologists)* is where Humes located an entry wound, near the external occipital protuberance, and stated that these fragments aligned with that entry wound. [3, p. 541] If Humes was correct in what he wrote, then this X-ray is a forgery, because such a line of fragments is absent.
- The notation, *entry (Clark Panel)* is where that investigative body located the entry wound: 4 inches higher.

- In addition, if an entry wound was where Humes said it was, near the external occipital protuberance, why isn't associated damage visible on the X-ray? Again, this X-ray is a forgery.
- The rear of the skull in the lateral X-ray is so opaque, it is "glowing" white. Based on David Mantik's work, the opaque area at the rear of the skull is much denser than what skull bone should be; it is a composite forgery. [70, p. 135]

Regarding the A–P X-ray, note:

- The 7×2-mm fragment identified in this X-ray was mentioned in the autopsy report. [3, p. 541]
- The circular 6.5-mm object, was not mentioned in the autopsy report. Therefore, it was not in the president's head during the official autopsy. There should be no doubt that if such a large fragment had been present, Humes would have found it, extracted it, and made note of it in the autopsy report.
- Based on Dr. Mantik's analyses, the 6.5-mm object was placed there after the official X-rays were taken. [70, pp. 126–129]

The incompetence of the forensic pathology panel cannot be overstated. This body of experts accepted the extant autopsy photographs and X-rays as legitimate representations of the wounds as they existed at Parkland Hospital, ignoring the fact that the contemporaneous reports by the Dallas doctors showed otherwise.

The panel also ignored important implications of the autopsy report written by Dr. Humes. With minimal study of the autopsy report, they might have recognized that when Humes wrote that the "scalp defect tears" extended in "stellate fashion into the more or less intact scalp..." [3, p. 540], he was describing incisions—incisions that he himself had made before the official autopsy. At the very least, Humes should have been questioned about this.

Perhaps more incredible is that the forensic pathology panel accepted as legitimate autopsy photographs that depict the back of the head as intact (Figures 34, 36). None of the photographs shows the segment of missing occipital bone that was described by the Parkland doctors (*e.g.* Figure

5). Moreover, Dr. Humes wrote that the head wound extended into the occipital region in the autopsy report. If the photographs in Figures 34 and 36 are genuine, they must have been taken after partial reconstruction by the morticians. It is inconceivable that the panel failed to question the authenticity of these photographs.

It is difficult to believe that the HSCA panel of forensic experts was so ill-prepared for questioning the pathologists involved in the autopsy. It appears that the panel members had done no homework, or that some were biased from the beginning, or even worse. They should have been well grounded in the Warren Commission Report, the autopsy report, the Parkland doctors' reports and all testimonies by the three pathologists to the Warren Commission. And, drawing on their expertise, they should have suspected that some of the photographs and X-rays, purportedly taken during the autopsy, were, at least, suspect. A complete discussion of this subject is available from David Mantik. [70]

Unlike the Warren Commission, who had been given a mandate by the Katzenbach memo, the HSCA had no such directive. It was free of restrictions, except those imposed by Robert Blakey who was running his own investigation unrelated to anything dealing with the medical evidence or the autopsy. From the outset, Blakey was principally interested in who shot the president and was hell-bent on trying to pin it on organized crime, his area of expertise. [68, pp. 8–9]

9.2.4. Wound discrepancies

The HSCA staff had difficulty in reconciling the fact that the observations by the Parkland Hospital doctors were at odds not only with the autopsy report but also with the extant autopsy photographs and X-rays. [71, p. 37] There was also the problem of "surgery of the head area" as reported by FBI Agents Sibert and O'Neill [20]. In Volume VII of the HSCA final report, they accounted for these problems in the following manner. Regarding surgery of the head area[14]—an observation that had been made by Dr. Humes early in the official autopsy—the report simply stated, "...yet no

---

[14]   Unbeknownst to the HSCA forensic pathology panel, the surgery to the head area had been performed illicitly by Dr. Humes (Section 4.).

surgery of the head area was known to have been performed." [71, p. 37]. Regarding the photographs, the report stated:

> In disagreement with the observations of the Parkland doctors are the 26 people present at the autopsy. All of those interviewed who attended the autopsy corroborated the general location of the wounds as depicted in the photographs; none had differing accounts. [71, p. 37].
>
> ...
>
> It did not seem plausible to the committee that 26 persons would be lying or, if they were, that they could provide such a consistent account of the wounds after 15 years. [71, p. 38]

These are misleading statements for which General Council Blakey must bear responsibility. It implies that 26 eyewitnesses to the autopsy[15], when shown the autopsy photographs, stated that the depicted wounds were consistent with their recollections. There follow six examples of witnesses to the autopsy who did not corroborate the general location of the wounds as depicted in the photographs; others interviewed by HSCA staff members could be included:

- FBI Agent Sibert, interviewed at home and not shown the autopsy photographs, told the HSCA that he observed the head wound to be in the "upper back of the head" (Figure 42), [72, p. 3] which is at odds with autopsy photographs showing the head wound (Figures 32 and 33).
- Dr. Ebersole, also an eyewitness at the autopsy, examining autopsy-photograph 42 (*i.e.* View #6, Figure 36) had the following exchange with HSCA staff member Andy Purdy:

> Ebersole: ...my recollection is more of a gaping occipital[16] wound than this...[H]ad you asked me without...seeing the picture...I would have put the gaping wound here rather than forward.

---

15 See Appendix III for the 26 names.

16 See Figure 4 for the location of the occipital bone.

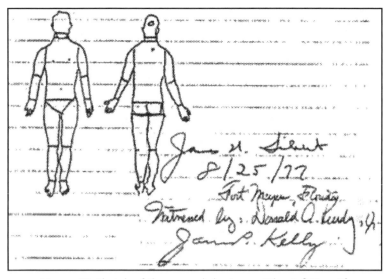

Figure 42. Sketch of the wounds by James Sibert. [72, p. 8]

> *Purdy: When you compare [Views #3[17] and 6], what inference do you draw now about the nature of the gaping wound to the President's head in terms of where it was located. Earlier you said it was in the back of the head. Looking at these two views, how would you characterize the location of that gaping wound?*
>
> *Ebersole: More lateral. Much more lateral and superior than I remembered. [73, pp. 62–63].*

- X-ray technician Edward Reed—interviewed by telephone and not shown the autopsy photographs—described the head wound as "located in the right hemisphere in the occipital region[16]." [7, p. 2]
- X-ray technician Jerrol Custer also was interviewed by telephone and not shown the photographs:

> *[When] asked about the persons present, the orders that were given, the types of X-rays, the photographs, the wounds, etc., Custer could not recall anything. [74]*

---

[17]   Figure 33.

- Gregory Cross, Lieutenant Commander and resident in surgery, also was interviewed by telephone and not shown the photographs:

  The only wound [I] saw was situated in the posterior aspect of the head. [75, p. 2]

- Jan Gail Rudnicki, a laboratory technologist assisting Dr. Boswell, who also was interviewed by telephone and thus unable to see photographs, stated that the "back-right quadrant of the head was missing." [76, p. 2]

It is remarkable that the HSCA considered the possibility that the difficulty in reconciling the wounds as seen at Parkland Hospital with those in the extant autopsy photographs and as described in the autopsy report could be reconciled in terms of body alteration:

> *The theoretical possibility also exists that both Parkland and the autopsy personnel are correct in their observations and that the autopsy photographs and X-rays accurately reflect the observations of the autopsy personnel. This could have occurred if someone had altered the body while in transit from Parkland Hospital to Bethesda Naval Hospital. This possibility however, is highly unlikely or even impossible. Secret Service agents maintained constant vigilance over the body from Parkland to Bethesda and stated that no one alter [sic] the body. Second, if such alterations did occur, it seems likely that the people present at the autopsy would have noticed them; in which case they are now lying about their observations. As stated previously, this does not appear likely.* [71, p. 38]

We view "Secret Service vigilance" as analogous to the fox guarding the chicken coop. [Section 10.2.] On the other hand, we now know that the statement above was correct in that the body was not altered while in transit from Parkland to Bethesda. [Section 4.] And we now know that the alterations were made by "people present at the autopsy." [Section 4.]

It is an omission of tragic proportions that no one drew a link between the possibility of body alteration—which had the elegance of a unifying theory—and the HSCA testimony of Paul O'Connor:

> *...the casket was a pink shipping casket and it arrived*
> *approximately eight o'clock...the body was in a body bag...*[10,
> p. 2, Section 2.1.2.]

In the final HSCA report, Mr. O'Connor's reference to a shipping casket is ignored although it *is* stated that the corpse was in a body bag. [71, p. 15] His testimony should have elicited searching questions since the HSCA staff must have known that the body was brought into the morgue in a bronze, ceremonial casket by the honor guard at 8:00 PM. [4, p. 1] They failed to question O'Connor on his certainty regarding a shipping casket, who brought in said casket, the body bag or his time estimate of 8:00 PM. Why?

Could it be that someone recognized the possibility of truly profound implications?

9.2.5. Blakey's *mea culpa*

The conclusion of *Section II. Performance of Autopsy* in Volume VII of the HSCA Report was as follows:

> *From the reports of the experts' analyses of the autopsy*
> *photographs and X-rays, the evidence indicates that the autopsy*
> *photographs and X-rays were taken of President Kennedy at the*
> *time of his autopsy and that they had not been altered in any*
> *manner.* [71, p. 41]

By maintaining that the autopsy X-rays and photographs were authentic, Blakey in effect lied to his own panel of forensic experts, including notables like Michael Baden and Cyril Wecht, who, perforce, arrived at erroneous conclusions about this evidence. They were deceived; however, they should have known better.

The final product of the HSCA, which consumed $5.5 million, is impressive only in its size: 686 pages with twelve volumes of appendices. [68, p. 8] In the final analysis, what did they conclude? Based on acoustics data, four shots were fired. The final report stated: [68, p. 6]

> *Scientific acoustical evidence established a high probability that*
> *two gunmen fired at President John F. Kennedy."*

Whom to blame? Organized crime.

In an interview with *FRONTLINE* in 2003, Robert Blakey issued a *mea culpa*. He admitted the CIA lied about "the case," meaning the JFK assassination investigation. In an addendum to this interview, Blakey listed a number of reasons for this assertion. He blamed George Joannides, a liaison between the HSCA and the CIA. However, this was much too late for excuses. [77]

The final product of the House Select Committee on Assassinations, like that of the Warren Commission, was a black hole filled with questions from which no substantive answers could emerge.

9.3. The Assassination Records Review Board

The key work performed by the ARRB was due to the efforts of Douglas Horne, chief analyst for military records. How he came to the ARRB in this capacity is described in his book *Inside the Assassination Records Review Board*. [32, pp. liii–lxxiii]

All researchers of the JFK assassination are indebted to what truly was the "last investigation": the work of the ARRB. Principally through Horne's efforts, salient facts about the assassination of President Kennedy have emerged. [32] It is ironic that, unlike the Warren Commission and the HSCA, the mandate of the ARRB was *not* to investigate or reinvestigate the assassination, but only to determine what documents produced during the assassination and its aftermath could be released to the public. However, by dint of his cunning efforts, Doug Horne convinced his superiors of the need to "clarify the record," leading to depositions or interviews of the following:

- The three autopsy pathologists;
- five Parkland Memorial Hospital doctors;
- FBI Agents Sibert and O'Neill;
- Autopsy X-ray technicians Custer and Reed;
- Autopsy photographers Stringer and Riebe;
- Chief-of-the-Day Dennis David;
- Petty Officer Saundra Spencer;
- Parkland Nurse Audrey Bell;
- Mortician Tom Robinson and co-workers at Gawler's funeral home.

With the exception of the autopsy pathologists, *none* of the other eyewitnesses was deposed by the Warren Commission, a shocking intentional omission. Had they done so, the case against Lee Harvey Oswald would have disintegrated.

The value of the work of the ARRB should be quite clear by what has been presented in this text. Through their discoveries of the accounts of Roger Boyajian, Dennis David, Floyd Riebe, Edward Reed, Jerrol Custer and Paul O'Connor, it has been established that the president's body went into the morgue via a shipping casket—in a plastic body bag—well before the arrival of the motorcade from Andrews Air Force Base. And from that crucial information it has been established that a conspiracy and cover-up occurred.

It should be mentioned that, as a result of his work at the ARRB, Horne has published a magnificent book [32] describing what happened after Kennedy was shot and why. Horne's book also presents a solidly based thesis that the CIA was involved in the assassination. [32, pp. 1628–1654]

10. Why President Kennedy was Assassinated

10.1. Underpinning Factors

To understand why President Kennedy was assassinated, one must go back to the early 1960s and examine the relationship between the United States and the Soviet Union.

Shortly after World War II, the United States entered a Cold War with former ally the Soviet Union. The Soviets had essentially enslaved millions of people in Eastern Europe, had established a temporary blockade of Berlin, and had built the Berlin wall. They were the "evil empire" well before President Reagan coined the term. The US government perceived danger to be lurking wherever Communism was in place or had significant influence, as appeared to be the case in Fidel Castro's Cuba. Moreover, we citizens were convinced of the dire threat of Communism.

In President Kennedy's first state-of-the union address, on January 30, 1961, he made note that:

> [I]n Latin America, Communist agents seeking to exploit that region's peaceful revolution of hope have established a base on Cuba, only 90 miles from our shores. Our objection with Cuba is not over the people's drive for a better life. Our objection is to their domination by foreign and domestic tyrannies. Cuban social and economic reform should be encouraged. Questions of economic and trade policy can always be negotiated. But Communist domination in this Hemisphere can never be negotiated. [78]

This was a bold pledge, perhaps one he should not have made. Whether he was serious or stated it merely to placate the citizenry and/or his military is not known. Nevertheless, he played into the hands of the CIA, whose plans to invade Cuba were formulated during Eisenhower's presidency. [32, pp. 1511–1512] Early in Kennedy's term in office, the CIA, most notably Deputy Director Richard Bissell, convinced him that an invasion of Cuba was feasible and that a popular uprising against Castro would ensue shortly after the invaders, all exiled Cubans, secured beachheads. This was foolish because Castro had the support of most of the Cuban people. [54, pp. 343–344]

Kennedy approved the plan and sanctioned limited air strikes to increase the likelihood of success. [54, pp. 346–347] However, National Security Advisor McGeorge Bundy (likely under the orders of the president) telephoned deputy director of the CIA Charles Cabell to say that air strikes were to be conducted only from an airstrip from a secured beachhead. The CIA wanted air strikes before the invasion. Secretary of State Dean Rusk, informed of the situation, offered to act as go-between so that the CIA could explain their view to the president; however, the CIA refused to discuss it. By not talking to President Kennedy, the CIA, in essence, canceled the air strikes with the expectation of forcing the president into committing the full force of the US military, which would now be the only chance of defeating Castro's forces. [54, p. 347] Kennedy's refusal to commit the US military resulted in a failed invasion and a humiliating defeat for the president for which he took the blame publically.

Furious with Allen Dulles, director of the CIA, and Bissell for deceiving him regarding the potential success of the invasion, Kennedy forced their resignations, five months later. As reported in 1966 in the *New York Times*:

> [A]s the enormity of the Bay of Pigs disaster came home to him, [the president] said to one of the highest officials of his administration that he wanted "to splinter the C.I.A. in a thousand pieces and scatter it to the winds." [79]

The CIA, in contrast to Kennedy's view, felt that the failure at the Bay of Pigs was the president's because he had not acted as they had anticipated. He vetoed air strikes before the invasion and the later use of United States military forces to aid the invaders. [80, pp. 14–15] Moreover, President Kennedy was perceived by the CIA and the military establishment as weak in the face of "Soviet aggression" since he had reneged on his pledge—to the American people, to the freedom-loving Cubans in Florida and to those in Cuba living under Castro's oppression—that a Communist nation would not be allowed 90 miles from our borders.

In spite of his "victory" over the 1,400 invaders at the Bay of Pigs, Fidel Castro had more to fear than before from the United States. Another invasion, this time by the full force of the United States military would easily defeat his army and remove him from power. Accordingly, he armed his country with Soviet missiles, which led to the Cuban Missile Crisis of 1962, when the two super powers stood at the brink of nuclear holocaust. (Note: Had there been no plans to topple Castro by "hit and run" raids on the island, followed by the Bay of Pigs invasion, it is likely that Castro would not have felt the need to arm his nation with Soviet missiles.)

Only through cool logic and determination by *both* leaders of their respective countries—President Kennedy and Premier Khrushchev—was nuclear war averted. Unknown to their military leaders, the two heads of government communicated through "back channels" and reached a peaceful settlement. The Soviets removed their missiles from Cuba and the United States removed obsolete missiles from Turkey that were pointing toward the Soviets. But one more concession angered the intelligence/military establishment: President Kennedy promised not to invade Cuba unless acts of aggression were perceived by the United States. [32, p. 1537]

The reader is reminded that the diplomacy President Kennedy employed to settle the Cuban Missile Crisis peacefully was considered admirable by most of the United States public. The rest of the world may have had a different view since it was possible Kennedy had created the crisis in the first place. The US intelligence/military establishment perceived that the president had "caved in" to the demands of the Soviet Union, which, to them, was the most despicable and dangerous enemy we had ever faced. The Soviets had gained a foothold in Cuba and would remain there as long as Castro was in place. President Kennedy had taken an oath to defend this nation which, according to powerful individuals in the military/intelligence establishment, he clearly had failed to do. This bordered on treason in their eyes. The plot to assassinate the president was likely in the planning stage at this point, and the death sentence may have been passed shortly after he delivered the commencement address at the American University in Washington, DC, on June 10, 1963, now known as the "peace speech." His words were aimed directly toward Premier Khrushchev, with a suggestion of *détente* with the Soviet Union:

> *[W]hat kind of a peace do we seek? Not a Pax Americana enforced on the world by American weapons of war. Not the peace of the grave or the security of the slave. I am talking about genuine peace, the kind of peace that makes life on earth worth living, and the kind that enables men and nations to grow, and to hope, and build a better life for their children—not merely peace for Americans but peace for all men and women, not merely peace in our time but peace in all time.*

Following this speech, the first "hot line" was established between the two countries and a Nuclear Test Ban Treaty instituted. [32, p. 1548] Perhaps Kennedy realized that the hard stance he had taken against Communism had worked against him.

The president's goal now was to enhance the relationship between the two superpowers because a most dangerous situation—the missile crises—had been resolved. Kennedy was also in the process of developing a better relationship with Fidel Castro, again through back channels. Through an intermediary, William Attwood, special advisor to the United States delegation at the United Nations, Castro sent word that he wished to come to a better understanding with the United States. [32, p. 1548] There should be no doubt that the sudden interest in developing better relationships between the United States, the Soviets, and Castro was an outgrowth of the Cuban Missile Crisis, which would have caused millions of deaths had it not been resolved peacefully. All three leaders realized the time for boastful, foolhardy talk was over; accommodation was necessary. On the other hand, in spite of these noble intentions, President Kennedy must have known he was playing a dangerous game by his efforts to enhance relations with the Communists without informing his State Department. These overtures by the president to the enemy were likely considered heresy by top officials at the CIA. [32, p. 1548]

10.2. Who Planned the Assassination?

President Kennedy's assassination was a classic *coup d'état*—a violent overthrow of leadership planned by a group of people. Who were these people? There is no evidence they were from a foreign nation. Therefore, they were from within our own government. Who was best suited, experienced, to carry out a plan to assassinate a president? What agency was most angered by the policies that President Kennedy had adopted—*détente* with the Soviets and Castro?

The Bay of Pigs invasion was a failure due to the president's decision not to follow through with what the CIA had anticipated he would do. And, even worse, Kennedy was perceived by powerful forces to have "caved in" to the Soviets in the resolution of the Cuban Missile Crisis. This was a nonsensical view since the United States traded with the Soviets; they took their missiles out of Cuba and we took ours out of Turkey. We still had plenty of missiles capable of reaching the Soviet Union from our submarines and bases in Italy. From the president's perspective, he had acted as a world leader in averting an all-out nuclear war between the superpowers. Moreover, he exhibited his disdain for the CIA who had deceived him in terms of assurances that the Bay of Pigs invasion would be successful. In effect, President Kennedy had declared war against his own CIA, while "appeasing" the Communists, placing himself in extreme danger. Thus, the CIA—or, at least, a rogue element thereof—is a prime suspect in the assassination of President Kennedy.

This possibility was first raised by Anthony Summers in his book, *Conspiracy*, [81] and confirmed by John Newman, who presented a solid case for this thesis. [82, pp. 613–637] Newman's work is also an excellent source for linking Oswald with the CIA. In agreement with Newman, Mark Lane's most recently published book is devoted entirely to an indictment of the CIA in the murder of President Kennedy. [83]

Although Summers, Newman and Lane each make a strong case for CIA involvement, the authors believe that the Secret Service also participated. The Secret Service controlled the motorcade route through Dealey Plaza, which provided a perfect setup for an assassination. They (Agent Roy Kellerman) took control of the president's body at Parkland Hospital, preventing a legal autopsy to be performed there. The Secret Service took control of the president's and Governor Connally's clothing immediately after the shooting, preventing key evidence to be examined until later. The Secret Service (Kellerman) had access to the bronze casket aboard Air Force One during LBJ's swearing-in ceremony and, we believe, removed the body and hid it in a storage compartment. Finally, Kellerman was instrumental in delaying the entry of FBI Agents Sibert and O'Neill to the

Bethesda autopsy, to prevent their discovery of the president's body there while the wounds were being altered. In short, the Secret Service stage-managed the cover-up.

It would be remiss not to mention also the actions/inactions of SSAs Kellerman and William Greer during the shooting. Based on the Zapruder film (Appendix II), Kellerman made no attempt to assist the president during the shooting. He remained transfixed, looking straight ahead. And if eyewitnesses can be relied upon, Greer either slowed or stopped the limousine during the shooting, in violation of protocol. [84]

11. Lee Harvey Oswald—The "Patsy"

The life of the alleged assassin, Lee Harvey Oswald, is discussed in meticulous detail in John Armstrong's book *Harvey and Lee*[18]. [54] Just a few facts will be taken from Armstrong's tome, which we believe show how and when Oswald was drawn into the planning of the assassination by the CIA. Oswald's journey from the Soviet Union to the Texas School Book Depository (TSBD) is key to understanding how he was set up.

11.1. Military Career

On October 26, 1956, at age 17, Oswald reported for duty at the Marine Corps Recruit Depot in San Diego. He was assigned to aircraft maintenance and repair duties [54, p. 147]. After serving at several camps, including those at Camp Pendleton, California, and Biloxi, Mississippi for radar training, Oswald was assigned to Taiwan in September 1958. [54, p. 200] He was granted a parental dependency discharge on September 11, 1959, nominally because his mother had not worked for almost a year due to an alleged work-related injury. [54, pp. 245–247] But Oswald's dependency discharge was a ruse. Eight days after his discharge, he boarded the *SS Marion Lykes*, which departed New Orleans for Le Havre, France, on September 20. [54, p. 251]

11.2. Soviet Sojourn

Details of how Oswald got from the United States to the Soviet Union—as well as the source of funds needed for this extensive travel—are not known; however, the last legs of his journey appear to be well documented. Allegedly, he left London on October 10, 1959, by air for Helsinki, Finland, where he stayed at expensive hotels. [54, p. 254] There, he applied for a visa at the Soviet travel agency, Intourist, for a guided tour of Moscow. A day later, his application was approved by the Soviet Consul, Gregory Golub. Such approvals normally required 5 to 7 days, yet Oswald obtained

---

[18]   *Harvey and Lee* [54] provides comprehensive proof that two people named Lee Harvey Oswald existed (Figure 41). In our reportage of what is a small part of John Armstrong's work, we focus on Harvey Oswald, the man who was murdered by Jack Ruby.

his visa within 24 hours. Armstrong proffers that Oswald had been advised by someone at the United States embassy (CIA) to contact Golub directly because there was, in effect, an agreement for immediate approvals of visas in certain cases. Apparently, our embassy told the Soviets to allow Oswald into their country. [54, p. 255] We believe that this was the beginning of the "setup" of Oswald.

Oswald's travel to the Soviet Union was for two purposes: he had to convince the Soviets he wanted to defect, and he had to convince officials at the United States embassy in Moscow—who were in the dark about Oswald's mission—of that purpose also. He arrived in Moscow by train on October 16, 1959. He was met by Intourist guide Rimma Shirahova, who drove him to the Hotel Berlin, where he registered as a student, claiming he didn't know a single word of Russian. This was false. The alleged assassin of President Kennedy was fluent in Russian. [54, pp. 265, 288] This had to be kept from the Soviets lest they suspected him of being what he believed he was: a spy.

Oswald's visa was good for six days. He tried to stay longer, but his application for an extension was denied. Apparently, he became distraught about this to the point that he attempted suicide. After being taken to a hospital for slash wounds on his left forearm, he was examined by a psychiatrist who concluded that Oswald had committed a "show" suicide. [54, p. 264]

Discharged from the hospital, Oswald visited the US embassy and met with Richard Snyder and John McVickar, who were led to believe he wished to renounce his citizenship (which, by the way, was never granted). Based on Oswald's tone, McVickar felt that he had been tutored, which might have occurred while Oswald was in the Marine Corps. Snyder and McVickar believed Oswald exhibited an unusual display of arrogance and an unfriendly attitude toward his country by threatening to turn over radar secrets and other information he acquired as a Marine radar operator. [54, p. 266]

Oswald was not stupid and must have known that his actions could have forced the embassy to arrest and detain him. But he wasn't apprehended and apparently had no fear that such would occur. He visited the embassy several times, and, according to a former secretary there, "Oswald had unprecedented access to areas that were allowed only to individuals who worked for the US in an official capacity." [54, p. 266] A possible reason for Oswald's "immunity" is that he was working for the CIA.

Oswald followed up his visit with Snyder and McVickar by writing a formal letter requesting revocation of his US citizenship. However, this letter was not sufficient for that to occur; a signed *Certificate of Loss of Nationality* was necessary, which he never submitted. [54, p. 267]

By January 7, 1960, Oswald was in Minsk, living in an apartment and under constant surveillance by the KGB. He had been given a job at the Minsk Radio and TV factory. [54, pp. 285, 286] In September of that year, he learned that the Marine Corps had changed his discharge from "dependency" to "undesirable." [12] This was to be expected for a former Marine who had announced his intention to defect to the enemy.

11.3. CIA Connection

By October 1960, eighteen United States citizens had defected to the Soviet Union. Some of them are known to have been double agents. An official at the State Department wrote to CIA Deputy Director Richard Bissell requesting information as to who were double agents. Bissell turned this request over to James Angleton's counterintelligence staff and not to the Soviet Russia division, which had jurisdiction over true defectors, counterintelligence-trained double agents, and false defectors. Since the request went to Angleton, it implies that Oswald was working under the overall guidance of counterintelligence, revealing his role as a double agent. [54, p. 306] Oswald's "defection" to the Soviets was a ruse.

When author John Newman asked CIA officer Robert Bennerman how the CIA's Office of Security responded to Oswald's "defection," Bennerman replied, "Jim Angleton (Counterintelligence) was in on this." Author Armstrong opines that Angleton and his staff were the people responsible for creating the "Oswald project." [54, p. 311]

In June of 1962, Oswald returned to the United States, well known as a defector who had expressed not only a desire to have his citizenship revoked, but also wishing to divulge secrets to the Soviets. The Soviets knew better. The authors believe the Soviets were wise to Oswald about his "secrets" from day one, which is why they did not wish to extend his visa for more than six days. His "suicide" attempt gave the Soviets some concern about what they should do with him. Obviously they decided to allow him to stay in their country where he could be watched.

Why wasn't Oswald prosecuted for his crimes upon return to the United States? He was separated from the Marine Corps by a fake representation; supposedly his mother needed him. At least ostensibly, he attempted to renounce his citizenship and threatened to divulge secrets to the Soviets, at the very height of the Cold War. The only possibility: Oswald was linked with the United States intelligence services. [54, p. 394] The authors believe that it was the CIA.

11.4. Back in the USA

On June 18, 1962, Oswald arrived in Fort Worth, Texas, where he registered with the Texas Employment Commission. On July 13, he was referred to Leslie Welding to start working. [54, p. 401]

On October 8, 1962, Oswald ended his employment with Leslie Welding and moved to Dallas. A few days later, he reported for work at Jaggars-Chiles-Stovall (JCS). Oswald's sister-in-law informed a neighbor that he was hired because he spoke Russian. [54, p. 415] JCS handled super-secret projects for the Navy Bureau of Materiel and the Army Mapping Service. [54, p. 416] Is this where a former self-proclaimed defector to the Soviet Union should have been employed?

On either August 2 or 3, 1963, Oswald passed out Fair Play for Cuba Committee (FPCC) leaflets on Canal Street, New Orleans. [54, p. 563] On August 16, he asked 19-year-old Charles Hall Steel to assist him in handing out FPCC leaflets in front of the International Trade Mart. [54, p. 571] What Oswald did not know is that CIA Agent William Gaudet watched him hand out this pro-Castro literature and that he was photographed by the FBI. [54, p. 564]

If the FBI and CIA were closely monitoring Oswald's FPCC activities, which involved a stated commitment to Castro, how was he able to assassinate the president? The point is that these activities, while appearing to support

Castro, were a smokescreen intended, in due course, to convince the public that he was a prime suspect for JFK's assassination. As Armstrong tells it:

> In the summer of 1963, on the streets of New Orleans, the setting up of Harvey Oswald as the "patsy" in the assassination of President Kennedy began. [54, p. 577]

One more step was necessary to entrap Oswald: he needed to be placed at a location where the assassination was to occur. On October 4, 1963, he was in Irving, Texas, at the home of Ruth Paine. He spent three nights there. [54, pp. 712–713] On October 7, 1963 Mrs. Paine drove him to the bus station in Irving to take a bus to Dallas to seek employment. [54, p. 713] Oswald was unsuccessful and on October 12, he left Dallas by bus for Irving, where he was picked up by Mrs. Paine who took him to her home. [54, p. 722] Two days later, on October 14, 1963, Oswald returned to Dallas. [54, p. 723]

On October 15, 1963, Mrs. Paine placed a call to Roy Truly, superintendent of the TSBD, asking him to hire "a fine young man"—Oswald [54, p. 725], who began working there the next day, October 16. [54, pp. 725, 727] Left to his own devices, Oswald had been unable to find employment. But with one phone call, Mrs. Paine landed him a job at the TSBD within a day! She was very involved in Oswald's activities during a time in which plans were being developed for President Kennedy's trip to Dallas.

11.5. Ruth Paine

Armstrong devotes a number of pages to her, with particular reference to her interactions with Oswald in 1963. It is notable that, 6 years earlier, while attending summer sessions at the University of Pennsylvania, she was a member of the Young Friends Movement, whose objective was to help ease East-West tensions. She studied Russian and, through the Young Friends Movement, made contact with Oswald via "pen pal activity." [54, p. 167]

Shortly after the assassination of President Kennedy, Mrs. Paine "found" incriminating evidence that allegedly belonged to Oswald. The details of the items are discussed in Armstrong's book. [54, pp. 509, 512, 514–515]

Most of these "findings" were used by the Warren Commission to indicate Oswald's guilt.

Armstrong reports that "undercover agent" Roy Frankhouser was scheduled to testify to the Warren Commission in 1964 about the Paines— Ruth and her husband Michael—but an order from the executive branch prevented the subpoena from being delivered because of "national security." In an interview with the HSCA, Frankhouser claimed Michael and Ruth Paine were also undercover agents whom he met when he infiltrated the Socialist Workers Party. He indicated that Ruth Paine became involved with Oswald in early 1963 as his intelligence "baby sitter" and assisted him in setting up a radical left-wing cover which included his one-man Fair Play for Cuba Committee activities in New Orleans[19]. [54, p. 524] The implication of this is that Oswald was likely told that the purpose of his fake pro-Castro activities was to infiltrate pro-Castro groups in order to discover their plans in regard to JFK. Perhaps this is how the CIA convinced Oswald to work for them—to gather information to save the life of the president: a noble objective.

11.6. Dallas Visit

On October 2, 1963, Governor Connally met with Dallas officials to discuss plans for the president's visit to the city. The authors believe that, with the publication of this information in the *Morning News* on October 5. [32, p. 1387] assassination plans were finalized. On November 8, 1963, it became public knowledge that he would be in Dallas on November 22. [32, p. 1394]

Since the specifics were then known in regard to the city and date, the planners of the assassination needed to know what route the president's motorcade would take from Love Field, as well the location of his speech to the Democratic Party faithful. Throughout the discussion, Governor Connally, the most outspoken, insisted on the Trade Mart. [32, p. 1392] The route chosen from Love Field to the Trade Mart included driving down Elm Street in Dealey Plaza, on which the TSBD was located (as would Oswald). To reach Elm Street from Houston Street, it was necessary for

---

[19]   Armstrong cites his source simply as "HSCA interview with Roy Frankhauser" [sic]. Caution is needed in interpreting Mr. Frankhouser's many and varied claims. [85]

the president's limousine to slow to a crawl to negotiate a 120-degree turn. This was a perfect scenario for an assassination: a slow-moving vehicle on a street overlooked by tall buildings with open windows. Such a dangerous route had never been taken by any previous presidential motorcade. Furthermore, security was minimized. The motorcycle escort was cut in half and Secret Service agents were not riding on the rear of the president's limousine, making the occupants a better target. [32, pp. 1397–1415]

12. Final Thoughts

Victory has a hundred fathers, but defeat is an orphan.
—Galeazzo Ciano

One might argue that fifty years of hindsight inevitably lends a clearer view of past events. However, the conclusions arrived at by the Warren Commission should have been known to be false immediately because the testimonies of key witnesses did not support the conclusions set out in their report. The single-bullet theory, for example was not supported by the observations of the Parkland doctors.

The "Lee Harvey Oswald as the lone assassin" thesis was assisted by the media and by the general public. The support of media gave legitimacy and strength to the falsehoods originated by the Warren Commission. Some of us remember a CBS-TV special—broadcast over four days—in which the dean of all broadcasters, Walter Cronkite, announced that the Warren Commission was correct: Oswald was the lone assassin. No doubt, many US citizens slept well on the night of the last broadcast, comforted by the assurance of the "most trusted man in America."

The public was guilty of unwarranted trust in their government institutions coupled with naiveté about President Kennedy. The Kennedy era ushered into our consciousness not merely a new, young, vibrant president, but what came to be known as "Camelot." And because of how we felt about him and his beautiful wife, we swallowed the official line: he was assassinated by a deranged pro-Castro sympathizer. The president's murder could not have resulted from a conspiracy even though there was evidence early on to indicate otherwise. The general public was handicapped by the sure belief that high-level conspiracies occur only in banana republics. We were a gullible nation.

The conspirators had a lot more going for them than they might have hoped. A compliant Warren Commission, a country deep in mourning, incapable of accepting facts, and media far too willing to bury their heads in the sand, all aided the conspiracy. Instead of Earl Warren, the country needed Sam Ervin; Arlen Specter should have been replaced by Sam

Dash. And the panel of forensic pathologists for the HSCA was seriously lacking as critical experts. Drs. Baden and Wecht had a chance to clear up problems in the medical evidence, but failed.

We will likely never know the killers of President Kennedy, *i.e.,* the shooters. We are now beyond that point. What we know (at least we should) is that the president was assassinated as a result of a conspiracy and that his body was altered to cover up where the shooters were located. We know beyond a reasonable doubt that Oswald did not kill Kennedy. The basis for this conclusion is solidly in place in the *Warren Commission Report* and in the twenty-six volumes of testimony. All one has to do is read these texts.

In College Park, MD, at the National Archives II, are official records related to the assassination of John Fitzgerald Kennedy: the autopsy report, the inventory of photographs and X-rays, the president's clothing, bullet fragments, bullet CE 399, and the Zapruder film. Most of these are not original or even copies of originals. They are, for the most part, forged and altered documents. They are like a cancer on the historic consciousness of this nation. They will remain there as the official records of the JFK assassination until the end of time.

Upon reflection on these facts, one can only weep.

Whatever thoughts one may have about all who assisted in perpetuating the falsehoods through the years, these authors believe—as did Sylvia Meagher, an independent JFK-assassination researcher who wrote in the magazine *The Minority of One* (1964)—that:

> [T]here are no heroes in this piece, only men who collaborated actively or passively—willfully or self-deludedly—in dirty work that does violence to the elementary concept of justice and affronts normal intelligence.

13. Appendix I
The Sibert and O'Neill FBI Report

Of those present at the autopsy on the body of President Kennedy at the National Naval Medical Center, FBI Special Agents James Sibert and Francis O'Neill were particularly important. They were the only non-medical eyewitnesses to write a report [20] on what they observed and heard from James Humes, chief pathologist.

One sentence in their report was particularly significant, indicating that surgery had been performed on the president's head prior to the start of the official autopsy at 8:00 PM.

> *Following the removal of the wrapping, it was ascertained that the President's clothing had been removed and it was also apparent that a tracheotomy had been performed, as well as surgery of the head area, in the top of the skull.* [20, p. 4]

According to Agent O'Neill, this sentence was uttered by Dr. Humes. [41, p. 70] What could Sibert and O'Neill have inferred from this statement? For one, that Humes was seeing the body for the first time; and second, that surgery on the head had been done somewhere else before the president's body arrived at the Bethesda morgue at 8:00 PM. Both inferences would be incorrect. Surgery had been done before the president's body arrived inside the morgue at 8:00 PM—by Dr. Humes himself (Section 4). The statement was made to deceive the FBI agents into thinking that he (Humes) was observing the president's body for the first time. This was false because Dr. Humes, as well as Dr. Boswell, was present when the shipping casket arrived at 6:35/6:45 PM. [86]

Notwithstanding the importance of the report by Sibert and O'Neill in terms of providing a truthful account of the official autopsy proceedings, it was less than truthful in describing their activities after their arrival at Bethesda Hospital. Their lack of candor was a direct result of having lost vigil of the president's body. As has been shown (Section 7.4.), their report was written to hide the fact that they failed to follow orders from

FBI Director Hoover. Their telling the truth would surely have resulted in at least a reprimand.

Notably absent from their report are important timelines concerning key events that they described. For example, no times are given for when:

- they arrived at the morgue;
- the bronze casket was taken into the morgue;
- the body was removed from the casket;
- non-medical personnel, including themselves, evacuated the autopsy room;
- those same personnel and they re-entered the autopsy room;
- the autopsy was concluded.

There was good reason for these omissions. Sibert and O'Neill were not present inside the autopsy room to make these observations and/or they fabricated them. Note, in the last paragraph of page 1 of their report [20], are the following sentences:

> *On arrival at the Medical Center...JACQUELINE KENNEDY and Attorney General ROBERT KENNEDY embarked from the ambulance and entered the building. The ambulance was thereafter driven around to the rear entrance where the President's body was removed and taken into an autopsy room. Bureau agents assisted in the moving of the casket to the autopsy room.*

One may conclude that the events described occurred sequentially with little or no lapse of time. For example, after Mrs. Kennedy disembarked from the navy ambulance, it appears the ambulance was then driven to the morgue, followed by Sibert and O'Neill. After arriving at the morgue, it may be presumed that the FBI agents assisted in moving the casket from the ambulance to the autopsy room, although the report does not state that directly.

There is one clue that the sequence of events did not occur as smoothly as indicated. There was some delay between the time of arrival of the motorcade and the time the navy ambulance with the bronze casket (empty) left for the morgue. The FBI agents used the word "thereafter," which connotes some delay. But for how long is not provided.

As a result of not including timelines, Sibert and O'Neill were able to conceal the following:

- There was a long period of time, over one hour, in which nothing occurred. The motorcade arrived at 6:55 PM, [39, p. 744] whereas, by their own admission, the Y-incision was not made until 8:15 PM. [20, p. 3] So, what was going on during that time period?: the "ambulance chase," [Section 6.5.] of which the two agents were unaware. However, perhaps they knew that by the date of their report four days later, which is why they omitted timelines.
- "Bureau agents" (*i.e.* Sibert and O'Neill themselves) did not assist in taking the bronze casket containing the president's body into the autopsy room contrary to what they claimed in their report. [20, p. 1] That was done by the honor guard at 8:00 PM. [4, p. 1]
- And contrary to their implied claim, [20, p. 3] we believe that they did not observe the removal of President Kennedy's body from the bronze casket.

  The President's body was removed from the casket in which it had been transported and placed on the autopsy table...

The wording is awkwardly in the passive tense. Had the two agents witnessed this event, the sentence would have read, "Bureau agents observed the removal of the president's body from the casket at (time?)," or words to that effect.

The report states:

...the first incision was made at 8:15 p.m.

However, even this statement is problematical. In his deposition to the ARRB, Sibert said that he didn't have a recollection of seeing the Y-incision made, adding that he did not know why he would have made that notation if it had not been the Y-incision. [42, p. 121]

If the FBI agents were not present in the autopsy room to observe the Y-incision, it is a certainty they did not see the honor guard bring in the bronze casket at 8:00 PM. When asked about the honor guard, Sibert could not "recollect" a military team present at the morgue. [42, p. 54] In contrast, O'Neill was certain an honor guard was present but *guessed* they were all from the navy, although they could have been from the army [42, p. 58], neither of which was the case.

Were Sibert and O'Neill active participants in the conspiracy and cover-up of JFK's assassination? The authors believe they were innocent of any foreknowledge to kill President Kennedy, and of the subsequent cover-up. Consistent with this is their disdain for the single-bullet theory. [25, pp. 176, 187] However, their failure to detail their activities comprehensively and truthfully in their report, an important document describing the evidence found during the autopsy, indirectly made them enablers of the cover-up.

They had a duty to perform: to maintain constant vigil of the president's body. When they assisted Kellerman and Greer, who were part of the cover-up, in bringing the casket (empty) into the morgue anteroom sometime after 7:00 PM, they should have insisted they have access to the autopsy room, regardless of what Kellerman told them. Had they done so, the history of the JFK assassination would have been much different from what it is today.

14. Appendix II
The Zapruder Film:
Another Altered Document

The Zapruder film (Z-film), named for businessman, Abraham Zapruder who exposed an 8-mm home movie of the assassination, has often been claimed to represent the best evidence of the events on Elm Street in Dallas on November 22, 1963. At the time the film was taken, it was credible evidence. Now it is not. It is a fraud, along with some of the most critical evidence stored today in the National Archives. How could it not be? If the body of the president was altered prior to the official autopsy at Bethesda because the wounds first observed at Parkland Memorial Hospital did not fit the lone assassin/Texas School Book Depository thesis, it follows *a priori* that the Z-film had to be altered. By the time of the official autopsy at Bethesda, the evidence that at least two shots had been fired from the front had been tampered with. Since the Z-film would not have supported the Bethesda observations, which were of an altered body, it had to be altered as well.

14.1. Eyewitnesses in Dealey Plaza

Fifty-nine eyewitnesses to the shooting were asked for their observations. Of these, approximately half said that the president's limousine either stopped or almost came to a complete halt during the shooting. Others expressed the view that prior to the shooting, the motorcade slowed perceptibly. None said the limousine accelerated until after the president was hit in the head, presumably the last shot. [84, pp. 119–128] The extant Z-film does not show the limousine coming to a halt or even slowing down. Hence, these frames have been removed from the original movie.

Is it possible that so many witnesses recalled an event that did not occur? The people who witnessed the shooting were there primarily to see the president and his wife, perhaps to wave, take pictures, or simply to be part of a major event: the president's motorcade passing through their home city. They certainly did not expect to see an assassination or to take mental note of the relationship of that event with the speed of the limousine. And yet they *remembered* the limousine slowing down or stopping with consistency as a collective body. And they recalled other facts with consistency, including where they were positioned along Elm Street, where the limousine was when the president was shot and how he reacted.

No one said that JFK's head and torso were propelled violently backward as depicted in Frames Z-313–326. Frame Z-313 supposedly corresponds to the instant of the fatal head shot. Is it possible that any witness saw the president being propelled back and to the left and forgot it? Sam Kinney, the Secret Service agent who was at the wheel of the follow-up car, saw JFK slump to his left. [84, p. 121] Zapruder's business partner, Erwin Schwartz, did not report seeing the backward head snap after viewing the film the next morning, November 23, 1963. [87, p. 327] And Dan Rather reported seeing the president's head go forward after the fatal shot. [87, p. 327]

It is reasonable to assume that Abraham Zapruder filmed the motorcade event from beginning to end. He told CBS News that he began filming as the limousine turned onto Elm Street. [88, p. 297] At the beginning of the film, Frame Z-1, Dallas police motorcyclists are making the sharp left turn from Houston onto Elm Street. In the extant film, the president's limousine is not seen until after making this turn; it "pops in" at Z-133 (Figure 43), representing a lapse of six seconds. Other anomalies in the film are described elsewhere. [89]

14.2. The Head Snap

Setting aside the fact that neither the eyewitnesses along on Elm Street, or the early viewers of the Z-film (Saturday morning, November 23, 1963) observed the violent backward movement of the president's head following the instant of the fatal shot, was it possible for such a backward movement to have resulted from a neuromuscular reaction, a "jet" effect or transference of the kinetic energy of a 160-grain bullet traveling at 2,000-plus feet per second?

Figure 43. Zapruder-film Frames 132 (upper) and 133.
[*Zapruder Film © 1967 (Renewed 1995) The
Sixth Floor Museum at Dealey Plaza*]

The answer is no for all cases, according to David Mantik. [88, pp. 279–285]
The neuromuscular reaction possibility was proposed by a ballistics expert
to the HSCA based on his "viewing old film of goats being shot in the head."
[88, p. 281] Mantik points out that no neuroscientists have come forward
in support of this possibility extending to the JFK assassination. Significant
differences in the neurophysiology between goats and humans tend to
discount a neuromuscular reaction as an explanation for the president's
backward head snap. In addition, the backward head snap is highly directional,
as depicted in the Z-film. Mantik cites the conclusion of Luis Alvarez that such
directionality would require "an *external* force." [88, p. 281]

A backward head snap from a bullet fired from the rear is possible, according to John Lattimer and Luis Alvarez, due to a jet effect. [90, pp. 248–259; 91] That is, the rapid forward push of tissue through and out of the cranium by the propelling bullet supposedly creates a force that drives the head backward (action and re-action based on physics). In their experiments, Lattimer and Alvarez, firing bullets through simulated human skulls, showed the "skulls" moving toward the shooter. Both sets of experiments, however, were seriously flawed according to Mantik. [88, pp. 279–281] Tests performed at the Edgewood Arsenal showed that human skulls filled with gelatin moved away from the shooter, contrary to the results of Lattimer and Alvarez, whose "skulls" were not anchored to another object as is the case of a human head connected to the neck, which, in turn, is connected to the upper torso. It should be noted that a backward movement of the head, as depicted in Z-313–326, required the neck and upper torso of JFK to be elevated (against the force of gravity) as well. It is not reasonable to believe that a bullet weighing only 160 grains, even with an impact velocity of 2,000 feet per second, would have sufficient kinetic energy to move JFK's body as seen in these frames. In any event, the final word should be that the backward head snap did not occur because no one saw it. Had the witnesses observed this dramatic movement, they would have remembered it forever.

The backward head snap is an artifact of the alteration of the Z-film. Frames near Z-313 were removed through the use of an optical printer. [92, pp. 139–144] For example, excising frames for the purpose of concealing a deceleration of the limousine (not seen in the extant film) would have the unavoidable consequence of "speeding up" an event. It is ironic that the head snap is viewed by many critics of the Warren Commission as proof that a shot came from the front, whereas that proof is derived from the observations of the doctors at Parkland Memorial Hospital.

Figure 44. Part of Zapruder-film Frame 337: a
"blob" obscures the president's face.
[*Zapruder Film © 1967 (Renewed 1995) The
Sixth Floor Museum at Dealey Plaza*]

There is another artifact at Frame Z-313 and subsequently, which, in this case, was intentionally added: the "explosion" of the head. These frames depict bloody matter that appears as a "blob," ejected from the right-temple area, above and forward of the right ear (Figure 44). It is likely that this apparent avulsion is painted-on artwork produced by aerial imaging, again through the use of an optical printer. [92, pp. 113–133] No eyewitnesses in Dealey Plaza saw this huge wound. Neither was it observed by the doctors at Parkland Hospital. But it has had the effect of convincing some people that it resulted from a shot from the rear, even though the trajectory was inconsistent with a shot from the TSBD. Moreover, blood and brain matter were blown backward and to the left onto Dallas Police motorcyclist Bobby Hargis, [11, p. 294] which is not seen in the extant Z-film.

Frame Z-313 also shows material propelled upward from the head, which disappears after one frame, *i.e.* within one-eighteenth of a second (Figure 45). Researcher John Costella concluded that if this spray were real, it should have lasted much longer. [93, p. 185] We believe that the spray and the blob were the work of special-effects experts; *i.e.* they were painted on, as was a uniformly black area over the rear of the head (Figures 44, 45). Note that in Z-313, Secret Service Agent Roy Kellerman is looking forward, having made no attempt to assist the president who had been shot several seconds previously. SSA Greer has turned around toward the rear. In Frame 314, SSA Kellerman is still looking forward. In Frame 321, both SSAs are looking forward. The president's head has moved a considerable distance toward the rear in only approximately a half second, the time interval between Frames 313 and 321. Frame removal would give the illusion that this movement occurred rapidly when, in fact, it did not.

Figure 45. Parts of Zapruder-film Frames 313
(upper), 314 (middle) and 321 (lower).
[*Zapruder Film © 1967 (Renewed 1995) The
Sixth Floor Museum at Dealey Plaza*)

14.3. Other Evidence of Alteration

In the extant Z-film—of which MPI's *Image of an Assassination* [94] supposedly represents the latest state-of-the-art version—there are identifiable missing frames and frames out of order. These represent the most obvious evidence of editing that resulted from cutting and splicing the original "out-of-camera" Zapruder film. There is the well-known Frames 207–212 splice, which, in 1967, *LIFE Magazine* (then the sole public owner of the film) admitted to and gave the explanation that a technician (unnamed) had damaged the missing Frames (208–211). There is another splice in the Frames 155–157 area, which no one has ever explained. And Frames 314 and 315 are reversed. These alterations were never questioned by the Warren Commission, the Secret Service, or the FBI. [95, p. 341]

There is also the matter of rapid head turns by SSA Greer, the limousine driver. Between Frames 301 and 303 and between Frames 316 and 317, his head turns about 150 degrees. The turn that occupies a single frame is much too rapid for a human head. In other places, such as Z-280–284 and 290–295, Greer's head turns about the same degree. Even these longer time intervals, equal to between a fifth to a quarter of a second, are too rapid for a human head to turn 150 degrees; strangely these rapid head turns are not blurred [96, p. 223]

14.4. Chain-of-Custody

The official version is that, after Mr. Zapruder filmed the motorcade events, the undeveloped film in its original 16-mm, un-slit format was taken to Eastman Kodak in Dallas for processing. (Note: the original film had two sides, A and B, each image path 8 mm in width. Side A contained a home movie of family and side B was of the motorcade.) The processed out-of-camera original then went to the Jamieson Film Company in Dallas for generation of three copies on a contact printer. These three exposed copies, went back to Eastman Kodak in Dallas for developing. Following developing, there was one original and three first-generation copies. Then, supposedly, Zapruder gave the original plus one copy to *Time-Life* for $50,000 the next morning, Saturday, November 23, 1963. This original deal gave *Time-Life* print rights to individual frames only for a period of one week. The other two copies were given to the Secret Service on Friday, November 22, 1963. [97, p. 480]

The next six pages contain Figures 46–51:

- Affidavits signed at Eastman Kodak and Jamieson establishing the authenticity of the original film and subsequent copies that were processed at their respective laboratories.
- The letter Zapruder wrote to Charles Jackson—publisher of *Time-Life*, who purchased the original and one copy of the Z-film— describing the chain of events related to where the original, out-of-camera, film was processed and where three copies were made.

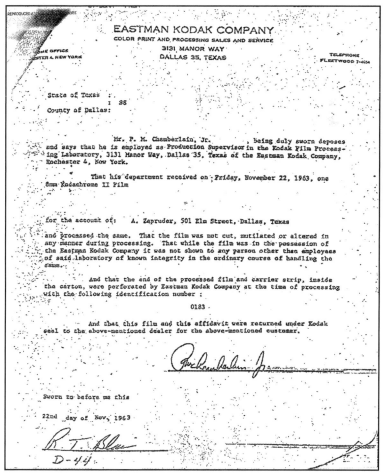

EASTMAN KODAK COMPANY
COLOR PRINT AND PROCESSING SALES AND SERVICE
3131 MANOR WAY
DALLAS 35, TEXAS

TELEPHONE
FLEETWOOD 7-4054

State of Texas :
: SS
County of Dallas:

Mr. P. M. Chamberlain, Jr.   , being duly sworn deposes
and says that he is employed as Production Supervisor in the Kodak Film Processing Laboratory, 3131 Manor Way, Dallas 35, Texas of the Eastman Kodak Company,
Rochester 4, New York.

That his department received on Friday, November 22, 1963, one
8mm Kodachrome II Film

for the account of: A. Zapruder, 501 Elm Street, Dallas, Texas

and processed the same. That the film was not cut, mutilated or altered in
any manner during processing. That while the film was in the possession of
the Eastman Kodak Company it was not shown to any person other than employees
of said laboratory of known integrity in the ordinary course of handling the
same.

And that the end of the processed film and carrier strip, inside
the carton, were perforated by Eastman Kodak Company at the time of processing
with the following identification number :

0183

And that this film and this affidavit were returned under Kodak
seal to the above-mentioned dealer for the above-mentioned customer.

Sworn to before me this

22nd day of Nov, 1963

D-44

Figure 46. Affidavit signed by Phil Chamberlain, Jr.,
production supervisor at an Eastman Kodak film-processing
laboratory in Dallas, with reference to development of a
movie film with the identification number 0183. [58]

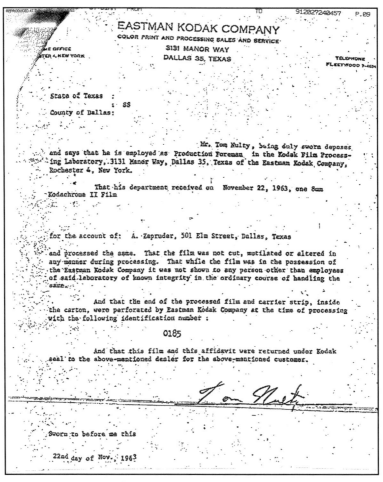

EASTMAN KODAK COMPANY

COLOR PRINT AND PROCESSING SALES AND SERVICE

3131 MANOR WAY
DALLAS 35, TEXAS

TELEPHONE
FLEETWOOD 7-4654

State of Texas :
: SS
County of Dallas:

Mr. Tom Nulty, being duly sworn deposes and says that he is employed as Production Foreman in the Kodak Film Processing Laboratory, 3131 Manor Way, Dallas 35, Texas of the Eastman Kodak Company, Rochester 4, New York.

That his department received on November 22, 1963, one 8mm Kodachrome II Film

for the account of: A. Zapruder, 501 Elm Street, Dallas, Texas

and processed the same. That the film was not cut, mutilated or altered in any manner during processing. That while the film was in the possession of the Eastman Kodak Company it was not shown to any person other than employees of said laboratory of known integrity in the ordinary course of handling the same.

And that the end of the processed film and carrier strip, inside the carton, were perforated by Eastman Kodak Company at the time of processing with the following identification number :

0185

And that this film and this affidavit were returned under Kodak seal to the above-mentioned dealer for the above-mentioned customer.

Tom Nulty

Sworn to before me this

22nd day of Nov., 1963

Figure 47. Affidavit signed by Tom Nulty, production foreman at an Eastman Kodak film-processing laboratory in Dallas, with reference to development of a movie film with the identification number 0185. [58]

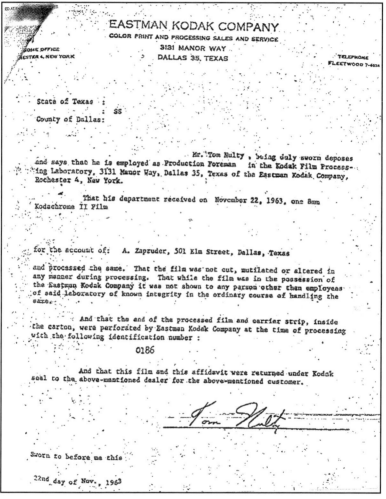

EASTMAN KODAK COMPANY
COLOR PRINT AND PROCESSING SALES AND SERVICE
3131 MANOR WAY
DALLAS 35, TEXAS

HOME OFFICE
ESTER 4, NEW YORK

TELEPHONE
FLEETWOOD 7-6634

State of Texas :
: SS
County of Dallas:

Mr. Tom Nulty , being duly sworn deposes and says that he is employed as Production Foreman in the Kodak Film Processing Laboratory, 3131 Manor Way, Dallas 35, Texas of the Eastman Kodak Company, Rochester 4, New York.

That his department received on November 22, 1963, one 8mm Kodachrome II Film

for the account of: A. Zapruder, 501 Elm Street, Dallas, Texas

and processed the same. That the film was not cut, mutilated or altered in any manner during processing. That while the film was in the possession of the Eastman Kodak Company it was not shown to any person other than employees of said laboratory of known integrity in the ordinary course of handling the same.

And that the end of the processed film and carrier strip, inside the carton, were perforated by Eastman Kodak Company at the time of processing with the following identification number :

0186

And that this film and this affidavit were returned under Kodak seal to the above-mentioned dealer for the above-mentioned customer.

Sworn to before me this

22nd day of Nov., 1963

Figure 48. Affidavit signed by Tom Nulty, production foreman at an Eastman Kodak film-processing laboratory in Dallas, with reference to development of a movie film with the identification number 0186. [58]

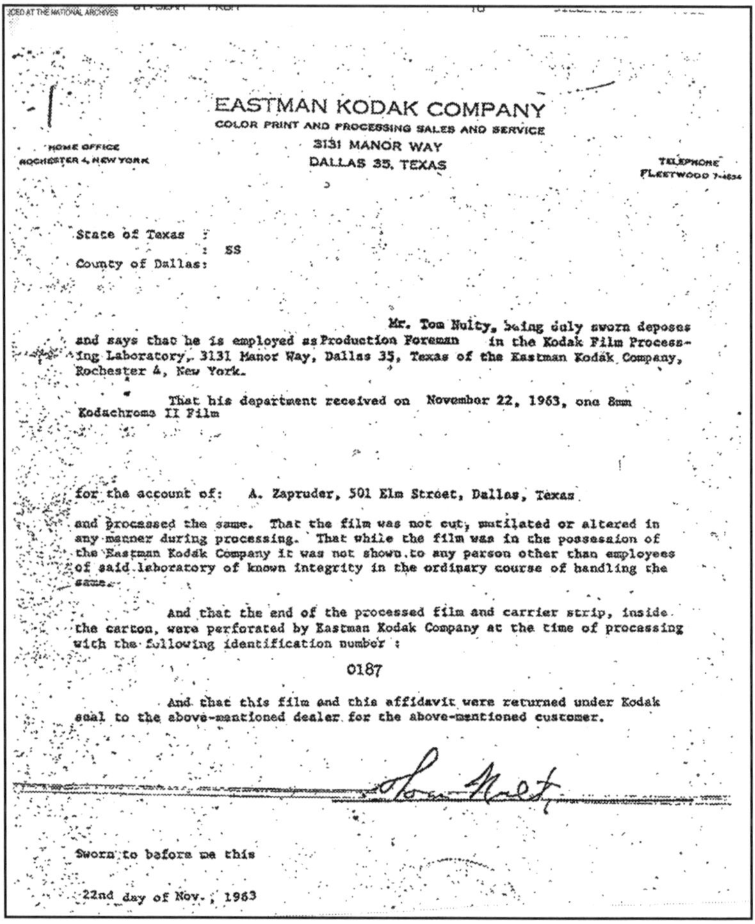

Figure 49. Affidavit signed by Tom Nulty, production
foreman at an Eastman Kodak film-processing laboratory
in Dallas, with reference to development of a movie
film with the identification number 0187. [58]

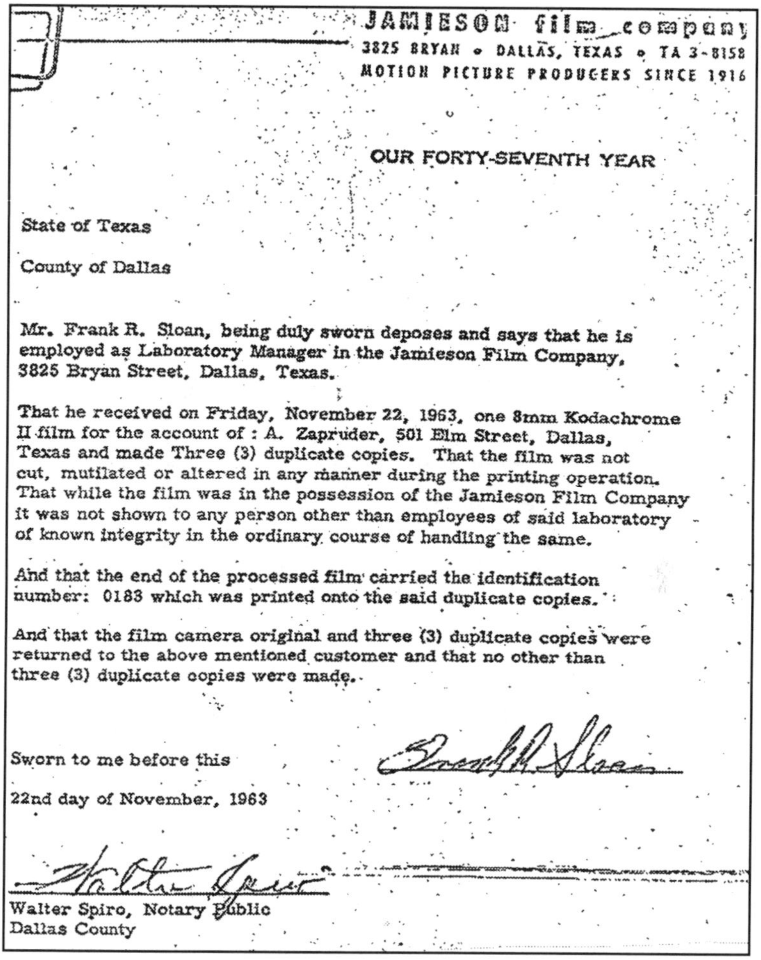

JAMIESON film company
3825 BRYAN • DALLAS, TEXAS • TA 3-8158
MOTION PICTURE PRODUCERS SINCE 1916

OUR FORTY-SEVENTH YEAR

State of Texas

County of Dallas

Mr. Frank R. Sloan, being duly sworn deposes and says that he is employed as Laboratory Manager in the Jamieson Film Company, 3825 Bryan Street, Dallas, Texas.

That he received on Friday, November 22, 1963, one 8mm Kodachrome II film for the account of : A. Zapruder, 501 Elm Street, Dallas, Texas and made Three (3) duplicate copies. That the film was not cut, mutilated or altered in any manner during the printing operation. That while the film was in the possession of the Jamieson Film Company it was not shown to any person other than employees of said laboratory of known integrity in the ordinary course of handling the same.

And that the end of the processed film carried the identification number: 0183 which was printed onto the said duplicate copies.

And that the film camera original and three (3) duplicate copies were returned to the above mentioned customer and that no other than three (3) duplicate copies were made.

Sworn to me before this

22nd day of November, 1963

Walter Spiro, Notary Public
Dallas County

Figure 50. Affidavit signed by Frank R. Sloan, laboratory manager at the Jamieson Film Company in Dallas, with reference to three duplicate copies being made of an 8 mm Kodachrome II movie film with the identification number 0183. [58]

Dallas, Texas
November 25th, 1963

Mr. C. D. Jackson, Publisher
Life Magazine
c/o Time, Inc.
Rockefeller Center
New York, New York

Dear Mr. Jackson:

This confirms the fact that I originally took the exposed roll of 8 mm. film concerning the death of President John F. Kennedy on November 22nd, 1963, in Dallas, Texas, to Eastman Kodak for developing and processing. At that time I requested Eastman to make three (3) additional copies, but was advised, firstly, that they were not equipped to reproduce these locally and that it would have to be sent to Rochester, and, secondly, that Jamieson Film Co. here in Dallas was equipped to make copies, so long as the film was not split but remained in the form of 16 mm. roll. Consequently, I had Eastman Kodak in Dallas process and develop the original roll of film without splitting the same, took such processed and developed film to Jamieson Film Co., and had three (3) copies made therefrom.

The laboratory manager of Jamieson Film Co. gave me an affidavit concerning the making of the prints, the original of which is attached hereto and is self-explanatory.

I then took the three (3) copies made from the original back to Eastman Kodak for their processing and developing. I was present during the times when the film was processed at Eastman Kodak and at Jamieson Film Co. and did not at any time notice or see any circumstance that would indicate that additional copies or prints of such film were or could have been made. I did not and have not authorized either Eastman Kodak Company or Jamieson Film Co. or any one else to duplicate, reproduce or in any fashion copy any of such film or prints thereof.

I am also delivering the originals of the four affidavits I received from Eastman Kodak to you herewith.

Very truly yours,

Abraham Zapruder

Figure 51. Letter from Abraham Zapruder to C.D. Jackson, publisher of *LIFE Magazine* describing the chain of events related to where the original, out-of-camera, film was processed and where three copies were made. [58]

Several important facts emerge from these documents:

- The original, out-of-camera, film (Kodachrome II) processed at Eastman Kodak was numbered 0183. This number was perforated on the carrier strip (at one end) of the film by the Kodak developing laboratory. The affidavit (signed by P.M. Chamberlain, Jr.) indicated that this original was not altered in any way; hence, it remained in its original 16-mm, un-slit, format.
- The affidavit signed by Frank R. Sloan, laboratory manager at Jamieson Film Company, confirms that the film received for contact printing was identified as 0183, from which three copies (and only three) were made.
- The three affidavits signed by Tom Nulty, production foreman at Eastman Kodak, confirm that he received three films (the three from Jamieson) for processing. Upon completion of his work, the three processed copies were identified as 0185, 0186, 0187. These numbers were, as was the number 0183 on the original, perforated on the carrier strip of each of the three films, respectively. Although not stated in these affidavits, the film used to make the three copies was Kodachrome II-A (indoor film).

Thus, sometime during the early evening of Friday, November 22, 1963, there was one original, out-of-camera, Z-film identified as 0183, and three first-generation copies, identified as 0185, 0186, 0187. A number is missing in this sequence: 0184. Perhaps another contact print was made at Jamieson and subsequently processed at Eastman Kodak in Dallas, but is not reflected in the affidavit trail. This would mean, however, that one or all of the affidavits is/are false. This raises the possibility of early access to the original on which alterations were made. [95, p. 409]

14.5. Alterations: Where and When?

In March 1976, researcher Paul Hoch discovered a CIA document, *Item 450*, through a FOIA lawsuit, which indicated that twenty-eight color photographs had been made of selected frames from "a Kodachrome positive of the Zapruder film." [95, p. 358] The document indicated that the work had been done at the National Photographic Interpretation Center (NPIC) in Washington, DC, shortly after the assassination. Prior to this discovery, there was no connection between the Z-film and the NPIC, a CIA-run enterprise.

In 1997, Doug Horne (ARRB staff member) interviewed Homer McMahon and Bennett Hunter, former CIA employees at NPIC, who had made the photographs described above. A summary of what Horne discovered is provided below; a full description is available elsewhere. [98]

An un-slit, 16-mm Kodachrome "original" Z-film was brought to the NPIC on either Saturday, November 23, 1963 (at the earliest), or Sunday, November 24, 1963 (at the latest). Both McMahon and Hunter said they were certain they made prints from various image frames before the JFK funeral, which took place on Monday, November 25. McMahon said that this film was brought to them by a Secret Service agent who identified himself as "Smith." Agent Smith told McMahon and Hunter that he (Smith) had personally picked up the film (in the undeveloped format) in Dallas from the person who shot the film. The film was never identified as or referred to as the Zapruder film. Agent Smith added that this film was first flown to Rochester, NY, where it was developed by Kodak, and then flown to NPIC so that enlargements could be made on NPIC's equipment.

McMahon told Horne that they had received an "original" because it was a "double 8 mm" and "we had to turn it over to see the image on the other side (side B) in the correct orientation." This account from McMahon raises serious issues about the chain-of-custody of the Z-film. A 16-mm, un-slit, film had been processed in Dallas on November 22. This second 16-mm, un-slit, film was processed in Rochester one or two days later, based on what Agent Smith told McMahon. There cannot be two "originals."

Both McMahon and Hunter were adamant about what they did that night, which—they were told—was to be treated as "higher than top secret." They made a number of prints (the exact number could not be determined) from selected frames of an "amateur movie." McMahon said the film was viewed as a motion picture four or five times during the analysis phase for purposes of determining "where the three shots hit." In addition to McMahon, Hunter, and SSA Smith, a co-worker at NPIC was present when the prints were made. McMahon did not identify this other person because he was still employed at NPIC.

After the analysis to determine in which frames "the three shots" struck the limousine's occupants, a minimum of twenty and a maximum of forty frames from the film were selected for enlargement, according to McMahon. Internegatives were made first, followed by multiple color prints of each frame.

McMahon and Hunter were told by Agent Smith that the color prints were to be used as illustrations for multiple "briefing boards," which were to be constructed somewhere else at NPIC from the prints. Both men were definite that, at no point, was the film reproduced as a motion picture. McMahon and Hunter made only internegatives and color prints of selected frames.

Based on the interviews of McMahon and Hunter, it can be concluded that the "amateur movie" they worked on was, in fact, the Zapruder film, but not the original as they thought or even a first-generation copy, in spite of it being un-slit. The film brought to the NPIC, which had been processed at Rochester, NY (according to Agent Smith), was a new altered/edited version. And the rationale for this conclusion is that the frames that McMahon and Hunter prepared for the briefing boards are—according to Doug Horne—"entirely consistent with what we see in the Z-film today." [99] Whether this altered film originated as 0184 (the one unaccounted for), or even the out-of-camera original 0183 shot by Mr. Zapruder, is not known. Whichever it was, it had already been altered, reassembled on an optical printer to create a "new" original film, and developed in Rochester, NY.

At one point during Horne's interview with McMahon, the latter mentioned "Hawkeyeworks" as the laboratory in Rochester where the film (brought to them that night) was processed. Hawkeyeworks was a classified code name for a top-secret facility run by Kodak for the US government. When the CIA discovered that one of its employees had used this term, the ARRB was notified that the name was still classified and had to be expunged from any audiotape of the interview, as well as deleted from any report.

In view of the CIA's sensitivity to the use of this name, it is plausible that "Hawkeyeworks"[20] was the facility at which the first altered/edited version of the Z-film was produced.

---

[20]   Horne never revealed the name "Hawkeyeworks" in any of his official unclassified memoranda at the ARRB. The name was published by an assassination researcher who obtained it from a separate ARRB source.

15. Appendix III
Autopsy Witnesses: Official List

During the autopsy, Special Agents Sibert and O'Neill recorded the names of what they believed were all the persons in attendance at any time. (25) In a report they submitted subsequent to the autopsy, they included: (26)

1. Adm. Calvin B. Galloway, commanding officer of the U.N. National Naval Medical Center;
2. Adm. George C. Burkley, White House physician to the President;
3. Comdr. James J. Humes, director of the laboratories of the National Medical School, Naval Medical Center, Bethesda, Md.;
4. Capt. James H. Stover, Jr., commanding officer of the Naval Medical School;
5. John Thomas Stringer, Jr., medical photographer;
6. James H. Ebersole, assistant chief radiologist at the Bethesda Naval Medical Center;
7. Floyd Albert Riebe, medical photographer;
8. J. Thornton Boswell, chief of pathology at Bethesda;
9. Jan Gail Rudnicki, laboratory technologist, assisting Dr. Boswell;
10. Pierre A. Finck, M.D., chief of the military environmental pathology division and chief of the wound ballistics pathology branch at Walter Reed Medical Center; (27)
11. Paul K. O'Conner, laboratory technologist;
12. Jerrol F. Custer, X-ray technician;
13. James Curtis Jenkins, laboratory technologist;
14. Edward F. Reed, X-ray technician;
15. James E. Metzler, hospital corpsman third-class;
16. Capt. David Osborne, chief of surgery;
17. Brig. Gen. Godfrey McHugh, Air Force aide to the President;
18. Lt. Comdr. Gregory H. Cross, resident in surgery;
19. Gen. Philip C. Wehle, commanding officer of the U.S. Military District, Washington, D.C.;
20. Chester H. Boyers, chief petty officer in charge of the pathology division;
21. Dr. George Bakeman, U.S. Navy (the committee could not locate this person);
22. Secret Service Agent Roy Kellerman;
23. Secret Service Agent William Greer; and
24. Secret Service Agent John J. O'Leary. (28)

(43) Through its own investigation, the committee determined that the following persons also attended the autopsy:

1. Richard A. Lipsey, personal aide to General Wehle; (29) and
2. Samuel Bird, (30) in 1963, a lieutenant stationed at the ceremonial duties office, Fort Myers, Va., 3d Infantry Division.

(44) Additionally, Sibert and O'Neill reported that, following the autopsy, four persons from Gawler's Funeral Home in Washington, D.C., entered the autopsy room to prepare the President's body for burial. They were:

1. John Van Haesen;
2. Edwin Stroble;
3. Thomas Robinson; and
4. Mr. Hagen. (31)

(45) These persons, together with Sibert and O'Neill, were the only ones present at any time in the autopsy room with the body of the President.

Figure 52. Official list of those present at the autopsy.
[71, pp. 8–9]

16. Sources and Notes

[1] Rinnovatore, J.V., Eaglesham, A. (2012) Aftermath of the JFK Assassination: Parkland Hospital to the Bethesda Morgue. Ithaca, NY: ARJE Books. http://www.manuscriptservice.com/Aftermath/. Also: http://www.amazon.com/Aftermath-JFK-Assassination-Parkland-ebook/dp/B007JM3AMW/ref=sr_1_1?s=books&ie=UTF 8&qid=1380377827&sr=1-1&keywords=Rinnovatore.

[2] Lifton, D.S. (1980) Best Evidence: Disguise and Deception in the Assassination of John F. Kennedy. New York: MacMillan.

[3] Report of the President's Commission on the Assassination of President Kennedy (1964), Washington, DC: United States Government Printing Office.

[4] ARRB MD 163—Cover Sheet Titled: "Joint Casket Bearer Team" (unsigned and undated) Containing time line of events, with report titled "After Action Report, Joint Casket Team—State Funeral, President John Fitzgerald Kennedy," dated 10 December 1963, and signed by 1st Lt. Samuel L. Bird, OIC—Joint Service Casket Team, attached. http://www.history-matters.com/archive/jfk/ arrb/master_med_set/md163/html/md163_0001a.htm.

[5] ARRB MD 177—Call Report Summarizing 2/14/97 Telephonic Interview of Dennis David. http://www.history-matters.com/archive/jfk/ arrb/master_med_set/md177/html/md177_0001a.htm.

[6] ARRB MD 236—Call Report of September 5, 1997 Telephone Interview of Roger Boyajian (Former NCOIC of Marine Security Detail at Autopsy of President Kennedy), With His Contemporaneous After-Action Report Attached. http://www.history-matters.com/archive/jfk/ arrb/master_med_set/md236/html/md236_0001a.htm.

[7] ARRB MD 194—HSCA Interview Summary of 4/21/78 Telephonic Interview of Edward F. Reed by HSCA Staffer Mark Flanagan, Transcribed on May II, 1978. http://www.maryferrell.org/mffweb/ archive/viewer/showDoc.do?docId=725.

[8] ARRB Deposition of Edward F. Reed, October 21, 1997. http://www. history-matters.com/archive/jfk/arrb/medical_testimony/ Reed_10-21-97/html/Reed_0001a.htm.

[9] ARRB Deposition of Floyd Albert Riebe, 5/7/97. .http://www.history-matters.com/archive/jfk/arrb/medical_testimony/Riebe_5-7-97/ html/Riebe_0001a.htm.

[10] ARRB MD 64—O'Connor-Purdy HSCA Interview (8/29/77). http:// www.history-matters.com/Archive/jfk/arrb/master_med_set/ md64/html/Image0.htm.

[11] 6WCH[21].

[12] Anonymous. The Assassination of John F. Kennedy Chronological Timeline. http://karws.gso.uri.edu/marsh/jfk-conspiracy/time.htm.

[13] Crenshaw, C. (2003) Let's set the record straight: Dr. Charles Crenshaw Replies. In: Assassination Science (Fetzer, J.H. Ed.) pp. 37–60. Chicago: Catfeet Press.

[14] 2WCH. (See footnote 21.)

[15] Thompson, J. (1967) Six Seconds in Dallas: A Micro-Study of the Kennedy Assassination. New York: Bernard Geiss Associates.

[16] Parker, B. (1995) A Conversation with Ronald C. Jones, MD. http:// www.jfklancer.com/parkland_drs.html.

[17] ARRB Deposition of Dr. J. Thornton Boswell, February 26, 1996. http:// history-matters.com/archive/jfk/arrb/medical_testimony/pdf/ Boswell_2-26-96.pdf.

[18] Livingstone, H.E.L. (1993) Killing the Truth: Deceit and Deception in the JFK Case. New York: Carroll & Graf.

---

[21]   6WCH=Volume VI of Hearings before the President's Commission on the Assassination of President Kennedy (1964). Washington, DC: United States Government Printing Office.

[19] ARRB MD 6—White House Death Certificate (Burkley—11/23/63). http://
www.history-matters.com/archive/jfk/arrb/master_med_set/
md6/html/Image0.htm.

[20] ARRB MD 44—Sibert and O'Neill Report on the Autopsy
(11/26/63)—"Gemberling Version." http://www.history-matters.
com/archive/jfk/arrb/master_med_set/md44/html/image0.htm.

[21] ARRB Deposition of Dr. James Joseph Humes, February 13, 1996. http://
www.history-matters.com/archive/jfk/arrb/medical_testimony/
Humes_2-13-96/html/Humes_0001a.htm.

[22] ARRB Deposition of Jerrol Francis Custer, October 28, 1997. http://
www.history-matters.com/archive/jfk/arrb/medical_testimony/
Custer_10-28-97/html/Custer_0001a.htm.

[23] HSCA Interviews by Purdy with Harper (8/8/77), Cairns (8/9/77),
Burkley (n.d.), Humes (8/10/77), Stringer (8/12/77 and 8/15/77);
document dated 8/17/77. http://history-matters.com/Archive/jfk/
arrb/master_med_set/md19/html/Image08.htm.

[24] ARRB MD 63—HSCA Interview of Thomas Evan Robinson, January
12, 1977, by Andy Purdy and Jim Conzelman. http://www.history-
matters.com/archive/jfk/arrb/master_med_set/md63/html/
Image00.htm.

[25] Law, W. M., Eaglesham, A. (2005) In the Eye of History: Disclosures
in the JFK Assassination Medical Evidence. Southlake, Texas: JFK
Lancer Productions & Publications, Inc.

[26] ARRB MD 233—Call Report of December 13, 1996 Telephone Interview
of Saundra Spencer (Formerly Stationed at NPC). http://www.
history-matters.com/archive/jfk/arrb/master_med_set/md233/
html/md233_0001a.htm.

[27] ARRB Deposition of John T. Stringer, July 16, 1996. http://www.
history-matters.com/archive/jfk/arrb/medical_testimony/
Stringer_7-16-96/html/Stringer_0001a.htm.

[28] Anonymous, JFK Assassination Evidence: Autopsy Photos and Xrays. http://jfklancer.com/photos/autopsy_slideshow/index.html.

[29] 3WCH. (See footnote 21.)

[30] ARRB MD 5—Handwritten Notes of Phone Call between Humes and Perry (11/23/63). http://www.history-matters.com/archive/jfk/ arrb/master_med_set/md5/html/Image1.htm.

[31] Livingston, R.B. (1998) Letter to David Lifton of 2 May 1992. In: Assassination Science (Fetzer, J.H. Ed.) pp. 168–171. Chicago: Catfeet Press.

[32] Horne, D.P. (2009) Inside the Assassination Records Review Board. Self-published; available from Amazon.com.

[33] ARRB MD 30—Testimony of Dr. Pierre Finck to the HSCA Panel, 3-11-78. http://www.history-matters.com/archive/jfk/arrb/ master_med_set/md30/html/Image00.htm.

[34] ARRB MD 45—ARRB Call Report of Interview of Jamie Taylor Re: JFK Autopsy. http://www.maryferrell.org/mffweb/archive/viewer /showDoc.do;jsessionid=530064E37E960473919F37 CB74DDE71E?docId=626.

[35] In a telephone call, Paul O'Connor was told that "someone took a ball-peen hammer to the head" to disrupt the wound and the physical characteristics of the wound. "[T]he body was...put back in the coffin and taken around the corner and down back of the hospital to the morgue." Livingston, H.E. (1992) High Treason 2, pp. 270-271. New York: Carroll & Graf.

[36] Deposition of Robert L. Knudsen to the HSCA, August 11, 1978. http:// jfkassassination.net/russ/testimony/knudsen.htm.

[37] Robert Knudsen's statement to the HSCA—that he became aware on the day after the assassination that photographs had been taken at the autopsy on the president's body [37, p. 5]—is in apparent conflict with what members of his family told the ARRB, *viz.* that

Knudsen had claimed to have photographed the autopsy [see page 4 of MD 230, http://www.history-matters.com/archive/jfk/ arrb/master_med_set/md230/html/md230_0001a.htm.

[38] Manchester, W. (1967) The Death of a President: November 20– November 25, 1963 New York: Harper & Row.

[39] 18WCH. (See footnote 21.)

[40] 7WCH. (See footnote 21.)

[41] ARRB Deposition of Francis X. O'Neill, Jr., 9-12-97. http://www.history-matters.com/archive/jfk/arrb/medical_testimony/Oneill_9-12-97/html/ Oneill_0001a.htm.

[42] ARRB Deposition of James W. Sibert. 9-11-97. http://www. historymatters.com/archive/jfk/arrb/medical_testimony/ Sibert_9-11-97/html/Sibert_01a.htm.

[43] Cullen, K. (1988) City Sailor Helped Carry Kennedy's Body. Danville: Commercial News, November 20. http://www.manuscriptservice. com/McHugh/Annan-2A.pdf.

[44] Cullen, K. (1988) Annan. Danville: Commercial News, November 20. http://www.manuscriptservice.com/McHugh/Annan-2B.pdf.

[45] Annan, R.P. (1993) Letter to the Editor. Danville: Commercial News, March 14. http://www.manuscriptservice.com/McHugh/ AnnanLetterBW.pdf.

[46] Rinnovatore, J.V., Eaglesham, A. (2012) "General" Activities at the Bethesda Morgue, 22 November 1963: Posthumous Words of an Eyewitness Lead to a New Theory. http://www.manuscriptservice. com/McHugh/.

[47] ARRB MD 153—FBI Internal Memorandum To: Mr. Belmont From: A. Rosen (dated 3/12/64) Summarizing, in Q and A Format, An Interview that Same Date of BUAGENTS Sibert and O'Neill by Commission Staff Member Arlen Specter. http://www.

history-matters.com/archive/jfk/arrb/master_med_set/md153/html/md153_0001a.htm.

[48] Brown, W. (undated) A Commission Without Commissioners: An Excerpt from The Warren Omission. http:// www.manuscriptservice.com/DPQ/wobrown-1.htm.

[49] 4WCH. (See footnote 21.)

[50] ARRB MD 2—Handwritten Autopsy Protocol (undated). http://history-matters.com/archive/jfk/arrb/master_med_set/pdf/md2.pdf.

[51] Zapruder film. http://www.youtube.com/watch?v=iU83R7rpXQY.

[52] Fonzi, G. (1966) The Warren Commission, the Truth, and Arlen Specter. Greater Philadelphia Magazine, 1 August 1966. http://karws.gso.uri.edu/JFK/the_critics/Fonzi/WC_Truth_Specter/WC_Truth_Specter.html.

[53] Jesus, G. (undated) Evidence Oswald Was on the 1st Floor at the Time of the Shooting. http://www.giljesus.com/jfk/alibi.htm.

[54] Armstrong, J. (2003) Harvey and Lee: How the CIA Framed Oswald. Arlington, Texas: Quasar, Ltd.

[55] Specter, A., Robbins, C. (2000) Passion for Truth: From Finding JFK's Single Bullet to Questioning Anita Hill to Impeaching Clinton. New York: HarperCollins.

[56] Salandria, V. (2012) Notes on Lunch with Arlen Specter on January 4, 2012. http://politicalassassinations.com/2012/11/1560/.

[57] ARRB MD 13—Signed Military Inventory of Autopsy Photos and X-Rays (11/10/66). http://www.maryferrell.org/mffweb/archive/viewer/showDoc.do;jsessionid=1345D50564B2394A040F198FBD2BE417?docId=594.

[58] Copied by JVR at the National Archives II, College Park, MD.

[59] ARRB MD 14—Review of Autopsy Materials by Humes, Boswell and Finck (1/26/67). http://www.maryferrell.org/mffweb/archive/viewer/showDoc.do;jsessionid=1345D50564B2394A040F198FBD2BE417?docId=595.

[60] Mantik, D.W. (2000) Paradoxes of the JFK Assassination: The Medical Evidence Decoded. In: Murder in Dealey Plaza (Fetzer, J.H. Ed.) pp. 219–298. Chicago: Catfeet Press.

[61] Clark Panel (1968) Review of Photographs, X-Ray Films, Documents and Other Evidence Pertaining to the Fatal Wounding of President John E Kennedy on November 22, 1963, in Dallas, Texas. http://www.jfklancer.com/ClarkPanel.html.

[62] Chudler, E.H. (2013) Brain Facts and Figures. http://faculty.washington.edu/chudler/facts.html#brain.

[63] Horne, D.P. (2000) Evidence of a government cover-up: Two different brain specimens in President Kennedy's autopsy. In: Murder in Dealey Plaza (Fetzer, J.H. Ed.) pp. 299–310. Chicago: Catfeet Press.

[64] Aguilar, G.L., Cunningham, K. (2003) Figure 9. Drawing of the Superior Surface of JFK's Brain. http://www.history-matters.com/essays/jfkmed/How5Investigations/How5InvestigationsGotItWrong_tabfig.htm#Figure_9.

[65] 17WCH. (See footnote 21.)

[66] Moyer, M. (1996) Ordering the rifle. The Assassination Chronicles 2 Issue 1, pp. 25–35. http://www.jfklancer.com/pdf/moyer.pdf.

[67] Twyman, N. (1997) Bloody Treason: The Assassination of John F. Kennedy. Rancho Santa Fe: Laurel Publishing.

[68] Fonzi, G. (2008) The Last Investigation. Ipswich, MA: Mary Ferrell Foundation Press.

[69] ARRB MD 21—Humes HSCA Testimony (9/7/78) http://www.history-matters.com/archive/ jfk/arrb/master_med_set/pdf/md21.pdf.

[70] Mantik, D.W. (1998) The JFK assassination: Cause for doubt. In: Assassination Science (Fetzer, J.H. Ed.) pp. 93–140. Chicago: Catfeet Press.

[71] Appendix to Hearings Before the House Select Committee on Assassinations (1979) Volume VII, Medical and Firearms Evidence. Washington, DC: US Government Printing Office.

[72] ARRB MD 85–HSCA Interview Report of August 27, 1977 Interview of James W. Sibert. http://www.maryferrell.org/mffweb/archive/viewer/showDoc.do?docId=347&relPageId=1.

[73] ARRB MD 60—Testimony of John H. Ebersole MD. http://history-matters.com/archive/jfk/arrb/master_med_set/md60/html/Image01.htm.

[74] HSCA Interview with Jerrol F. Custer 6/19/78. http://kenrahn.com/Marsh/Jfk-conspiracy/CUSTER.TXT

[75] HSCA Interview with Gregory Cross 04/24/78. http://kenrahn.com/Marsh/HSCA/CROSS_G.TXT

[76] HSCA Interview with Jan Rudnicki 5/8/78. HSCA rec. # 180-10105-10397, agency file number # 014461, p. 2.

[77] FRONTLINE Interview: G. Robert Blakey (2003). http://www.pbs.org/wgbh/pages/frontline/shows/oswald/interviews/blakey.html.

[78] Kennedy, J.F. (1961) State of the Union 1961. http://www.let.rug.nl/usa/presidents/john-fitzgerald-kennedy/state-of-the-union-1961.php.

[79] Wicker, T. *et al.* (1966) C.I.A.: Maker of policy or tool? New York Times April 25, p. 20.

[80] Douglass, J. (2008) JFK and the Unspeakable: Why He Died and Why it Matters. New York: Orbis.

[81] Summers, A. (1980) Conspiracy. New York: McGraw-Hill.

[82] Newman, J. (2008) Oswald and the CIA: The Documented Truth About the Unknown Relationship Between the U.S. Government and the Alleged Killer of JFK. New York: Skyhorse Publishing.

[83] Lane, M. (2011) Last Word: My Indictment of the CIA in the Murder of JFK. New York: Skyhorse Publishing.

[84] Palamara, V. (2000) 59 Witnesses: Delay on Elm Street. In: Murder in Dealey Plaza (Fetzer, J.H. Ed.) pp. 119–128. Chicago: Catfeet Press. http://www.acorn.net/jfkplace/09/fp.back_issues/27th_Issue/59_1.html.

[85] Anonymous. Palimpsest World: The Serpentine Trail of Roy Frankhouser from the SWP, the KKK, and the "Knights of Malta" to Far Beyond the Grassy Knoll. http://laroucheplanet.info/pmwiki/downloads/PALIMPSEST%20WORLD.pdf.

[86] Rinnovatore, J. (2011) JFK 11/22/63: Body/Casket Chicanery at the Bethesda Morgue. http://www.manuscriptservice.com/BNH-chicanery/.

[87] Mantik, D.W. (2000) Paradoxes of the JFK assassination: The Zapruder film controversy. In: Murder in Dealey Plaza (Fetzer, J.H. Ed.) pp. 325–360. Chicago: Catfeet Press.

[88] Mantik, D.W. (1998) Special effects in the Zapruder film: How the film of the century was edited. In: Assassination Science (Fetzer, J.H. Ed.) pp. 263–344. Chicago: Catfeet Press.

[89] Fetzer, J.H. (Ed.) (2003) The Great Zapruder Film Hoax: Deceit and Deception in the Death of JFK. Chicago: Catfeet Press.

[90] Lattimer, J.K. (1980) Kennedy and Lincoln: Medical and Ballistic Comparisons of their Assassinations. New York: Harcourt Brace Jovanovich.

[91] Alvarez, L.W. (1976) A physicist examines the Kennedy assassination film. American Journal of Physics 44, pp. 813–827.

[92] Healy, D. (2003) Part II: Technical aspects of film alteration. In: The Great Zapruder Film Hoax: Deceit and Deception in the Death of JFK (Fetzer, J.H. Ed.) pp. 113–144. Chicago: Catfeet Press.

[93] Costella, J. (2003) A scientist's verdict: The film is a fabrication. In: The Great Zapruder Film Hoax: Deceit and Deception in the Death of JFK (Fetzer, J.H. Ed.) pp. 145–221. Chicago: Catfeet Press.

[94] Motyl, H.D. *et al.* (1998) Image of an Assassination: A New Look at the Zapruder Film (DVD). Orland Park: MPI Home Video.

[95] Lifton, D.S. (2003) Pig on a leash: A question of authenticity. In: The Great Zapruder Film Hoax: Deceit and Deception in the Death of JFK (Fetzer, J.H. Ed.) pp. 309–426. Chicago, Catfeet Press.

[96] Pincher, M., Schaeffer, R.L. (1998) The case for Zapruder film tampering: The blink pattern. In: Assassination Science (Fetzer, J.H. Ed.) pp. 221–238. Chicago: Catfeet Press.

[97] Lifton, D.S. (2003) Appendix H: Lifton on the Zavada report. In: The Great Zapruder Film Hoax: Deceit and Deception in the Death of JFK (Fetzer, J.H. Ed.) pp. 479–482. Chicago, Catfeet Press.

[98] Horne, D.P. (2012) The Two NPIC Zapruder Film Events: Signposts Pointing to the Film's Alteration. http://www.manuscriptservice. com/NPIC-DougHorne/.

[99] Horne, D.P. (2005) Email, November 2.

---

17. Section Index